Enacting Love:

How Thomas Merton Died for Peace

What Readers Are Saying:

"In early summer of 2015, I received a phone call, totally out of the blue, from a gentleman wanting to visit the Merton Center and who had an astonishing story he was bursting to share, most especially with someone like myself who would understand the unique significance of that remarkable story. So it was that in late July 2015 John Smelcer walked, almost bounced, I have to say, he was so wired with excitement and anticipation, into the Merton Center and into my life." –Dr. Paul Pearson, Director of the Thomas Merton Center (from the Foreword)

"John Smelcer has faithfully told my story and that of my late husband and our beloved friend and brother in Christ, Thomas Merton." –Helen Marie Grimes (formerly Sister Mary Pius)

"For more than fifty years, I and many have lived with the suspicion that Thomas Merton, like his friend Martin Luther King, Jr., died a martyr. This amazing and thoroughly documented book that reads like a detective story reveals a startling twist in the story, confirming what I have long believed: The answer is Yes. The meaning is for all to ponder." –Matthew Fox, author of *Original Blessing* and *A Way to God: Thomas Merton's Creation Spirituality Journey*

"Thomas Merton's premonitions about his assassination are not proof that they were fulfilled, but I find them deeply moving—and so will readers. I remember him saying at Redwoods Abbey just before he departed on his fateful journey to Asia, "Pray for me. This is dangerous." At the time, we thought he simply meant the usual dangers of exotic travel." –Br. David Steindl-Rast, Benedictine monk, author, and friend of Thomas Merton

"I was sitting in a coffee house at Notre Dame when I read the news that Thomas Merton had died. Even then, I was suspicious about his death." –Fr. Emmanuel Charles McCarthy

"A. J. Heschel, my mentor at the Jewish Theological Seminary, loved Merton's work and introduced me to his writings. Here was an ally to Jews who were at the time hoping that the Catholic Church would go beyond eliminating the Church's teaching of hatred toward Jews and require every parish to teach its children about the way Christianity had been a major force in developing hatred of Jews. It was only later, as a social change activist that I found Merton to be a great inspiration for all of us who sought to heal and transform the world. *Enacting Love* reminds us of how very much we lost in Merton's probable assassination, just as we lost Martin Luther King, Jr. and Bobby Kennedy that same year. His writings continue to make him a welcome ally to all of us involved in trying to build a society of love and justice." –Rabbi Michael Lerner, Editor of *Tikkun*

"If you ask me, what Smelcer suggests in this book is not at all out of the realm of possibility." –Marc Becker, author of *The C.I.A. in Ecuador* and *The F.B.I. in Latin America*

Enacting Love:
How Thomas Merton Died for Peace

By
John Smelcer

Foreword by Dr. Paul Pearson, Director
Thomas Merton Center at Bellarmine University

Naciketas Press
715 E. McPherson
Kirksville, Missouri 63501
2022

Enacting Love: How Thomas Merton Died for Peace
©2022 John Smelcer
Cover photograph used with permission of the Thomas Merton Trust.
Cover design by Rusty Nelson.

All rights reserved. No part of this book may be reproduced without permission from the author or publisher, except in the case of brief excerpts as part of critical reviews.

A portion of the royalties from the sales of this book will be donated to the Thomas Merton Center at Bellarmine University.

ISBN   978-1-952232-67-1

Library of Congress Control Number: 2021950633

Published by:
    Naciketas Press
    715 E. McPherson
    Kirksville, Missouri 63501

Available at:
    Nitai's Bookstore
    715 E. McPherson
    Kirksville, Missouri, 63501
    Phone: (660) 665-0273
    http://www.nitaisbookstore.com
    http://www.naciketas-press.com
    Email: neal@blazing-sapphire-press.com

for Thomas Merton and his brother and sister in Christ—
Robert and Helen Marie Grimes
(formerly Brother Irenaeus and Sister Mary Pius)

"Blessed are the peacemakers, for they
will be called the children of God." (Matthew 5:9)

"Greater love has no one than this:
to lay down one's life for friends." (John 15:13)

"The unforgivable default of our society has been its failure to apprehend the assassins." Martin Luther King, Jr., *Why We Can't Wait*

Acknowledgements

Excerpts, in the form of articles, from this book were first published in *Tikkun, Ragazine, Rosebud, Bellarmine, Kentucky Monthly, Thomas Merton Seasonal*, and in blogs for the Charter for Compassion.

The author would like to thank his wife, Amber Johnson, for enduring countless discussions about Thomas Merton and for coming up with the title of this book. He would also like to thank Helen Marie Grimes (aka Sister Mary Pius), Jack W., Dan Johnson, Carita Trent, Steve McDuff, Br. David Steindl-Rast, Matthew Fox, James W. Douglass, Emmanuel Charles McCarthy, Fr. Leo Walsh, Maria Dammer Jägerstätter, James O'Donnell, Robert Dager, Dale Stone, Rabbi Michael Lerner, Neal and Betsy Delmonico, Jon and Jane Waddington, Rusty Nelson, and Marc Becker. The author wishes to express a special debt of gratitude to Dr. Paul Pearson, director of the Thomas Merton Center at Bellarmine University, for his generous assistance and contributions to this book.

Contents

Paul Pearson: Foreword vii
    New Discoveries vii
    The Humility of Merton xii
    Centenary Exhibit xiii

The Most Famous Monk in the World   3

The Assassination of Thomas Merton   15

The Monk Who Fell From the Sky   29

The Intrepid Little Nun   53

The Abbot's Orders   85

The Abbot's Homily for Thomas Merton   89

A Nun and a Monk Walk into a Wedding Chapel   101

The Pilfering of the Thomas Merton Collection (1970-2015)   115

The Right Place at the Right Time   127

The Naysayers	135
Abbey of Gethsemani or Bust	149
Easy Come, Easy Go	167
Franz Jägerstätter: Merton's Model of Moral Courage	173
Enacting Love	185
A Distillation of Faith	193
Absolute Power Corrupts Absolutely	205
Pieces of a Puzzle	215
Afterword	223
Works Cited	235
About the Authors	241

Paul Pearson: Foreword

New Discoveries

I am now in my twentieth year as director of the Thomas Merton Center, and during that time there have been some memorable events that have happened including the 40th anniversary of the starting of the collection, the centenary of Merton's birth and the 50th anniversary of his death. But one of the highlights for me personally over the years has been some of the remarkable donations and acquisitions to the Center's already extensive collections, most notably:

- the Merton papers of Robert Giroux, Merton's friend and editor who oversaw Merton's literary ascendancy with his editing of *The Seven Storey Mountain*.

- a collection of Merton's calligraphies that had been sent to the abstract artist, Ad Reinhardt, which would be donated by Reinhardt's family.

- largely through purchase, the development of the largest public collection of Owen Merton's paintings in the world. Fulfilling a vision Merton himself had shared with one of his New Zealand aunts of bringing together an exhibit of his father's paintings, with the paintings eventually residing at the Thomas Merton Center.

- the Merton papers of Merton's friend and literary trustee, Tommie O'Callaghan.
- the *Catholic Worker* and Dorothy Day papers of Joseph Zarrella.
- other collections from a variety of Merton's friends, correspondents, and private collectors too numerous to list here.

It is remarkable how, over fifty years since Merton's death, new materials still continue to come to light. Most recently, the Center purchased an original letter from Merton to Lewis Mumford that predated any correspondence that we had in the collection between them; original correspondence between Merton and Peter Geist concerning the publication of *Monastic Life at Gethsemani* was donated; and a more unusual artifact, an empty Mateus Rose bottle from a 1967 picnic with Tommie O'Callaghan and Sr. Therese Lentfoehr. (Sr. Therese was one of the earliest collectors of Merton's artifacts. She was aware of his poetry even before his entry to Gethsemani, having first written to him in 1939. She kept the empty bottle from the picnic as a souvenir and, through a well-documented but circuitous route, it eventually found its way back to Kentucky!)

Which brings me to another extraordinary collection donated to the Merton Center in recent years, a collection which is the linchpin for the book you are holding. In early summer of 2015, I received a phone call, totally out of the blue, from a gentleman wanting to visit the Merton Center, who had an astonishing story he was bursting to share, most especially with someone like myself who would understand the unique significance of that remarkable story. So it was that in late July 2015, Dr. John Smelcer walked, almost bounced, I have to say, he was so wired with excitement and anticipation, into the

Paul Pearson: Foreword

Merton Center and into my life.

 The story he proceeded to share with me is recounted in the pages of this book, so I will not ruin his story for you, but perhaps just whet your appetite with anticipation! Through another circuitous route a number of items of Thomas Merton's clothing, along with some other artifacts, had been entrusted to John by their owner for him to find the appropriate home for them. John had traveled to Louisville by motorcycle from Northern Missouri and so was unable to bring any of the items with him, though he did have ample digital photographs to share. A few weeks later we made arrangements for me to visit Missouri to view the collection of artifacts in John's possession and to safely bring them back to the Thomas Merton Center where they could be preserved for future generations and exhibited for visitors to the Center.

 Upon my arrival, without any further ado, John immediately took me to see the trunks of clothing. We opened the first trunk and, strategically placed, as John later told me, there was Thomas Merton's iconic denim work jacket that is seen in numerous famous photographs of him, most noticeably those of Ed Rice and John Lyons. I have seen photographs of that jacket so often, and I remember numerous conversations with Fr. Alan Gilmore, OCSO who was in charge of the laundry at Gethsemani in the sixties and who had supplied Merton with the jacket from the "common box."

 In the photographs of Merton in this jacket there is a "design" on one lapel of the collar. When I'd first seen it I thought it was some kind of Chinese character or ideogram. Fr. Alan, in one of our conversations, explained that the jacket was in fact a "hand-me-down" from another monk who had either died or who had left the monastery. When clothing was returned, the deceased monk's laundry number was scratched out and the laundry number of the next monk to whom the clothing was issued was written beside or below it. If you look carefully at photographs of Merton in that jacket you will see that he was, in fact, the third monk to have "owned" this jacket. The laundry numbers of two former monks had been scratched and Merton's laundry number, 127, written beneath it. Fr. Alan often joked that if he'd realized the jacket would be immortalized by the photographs of Merton wearing it he would have given Merton a newer one in better condition!

So, having seen these photographs, having heard this history from Fr. Alan, and having asked numerous monks and friends of Merton if they knew what had happened to this jacket, here, at long last, it was— folded in the trunk right in front of me. As I knelt down—not out of reverence, but because the trunk was on the floor—it was a quite extraordinary, emotional moment for me. Although, at that time, I had been director of the Merton Center for fifteen years and had written academically about Merton and attended conferences since the 1980's, that wasn't the Merton I'd first encountered as a teenager in England. Like the majority of Merton's readers I was drawn to his extraordinary ability to write about the spiritual, in particular the intrinsic relationship of contemplation and action, in a way that was accessible, meaningful, powerful, and, for many including myself, life changing. As one Episcopal bishop had written, Merton's autobiography was one of those rare books that "read me, as much as I read it." My own personal encounter with this Merton would continue alongside my academic and professional interest.

A unique moment came for me when in May 1989. I was able to attend the first general meeting of the International Thomas Merton Society held at Bellarmine College in Louisville. This was my first ever visit to the United States and, on that visit, as well as attending the Merton conference, I was able to visit the Merton Center, then in the basement of St. Bonaventure's Hall on the Bellarmine campus, and the Abbey of Gethsemani and Merton's hermitage. The whole trip was a remarkable experience, a pilgrimage, in which I was drawn into a circle that Merton himself would call his "apostolate of friendship." All these factors would eventually coalesce in the uprooting of myself and my young family from our home in London to Louisville to direct the Merton Center.

Dear Reader, hopefully against this background of my own experience with Merton over a number of decades, you might be able to imagine the emotion I felt in seeing, indeed, in holding in my own hands, this iconic item of Merton's clothing that had been hidden from the world since Merton's death in 1968. As John writes in this book, that moment led to tears running down my cheeks. Not from any single emotion that I could identify but from the culmination of my own journey with Merton to this moment when, with that jacket held out before me, it was like having the physical embodiment of Merton standing in front of me. As visitors to the Merton Center can testify, I spend my days surrounded by numerous images of Merton. Probably a day doesn't pass without my reading something of his, or without his name passing my lips. I am sure others have some inkling of this emotion felt when, having read Merton their whole life, they visit the Merton Center for the first time, or stand at the corner of Fourth and Walnut, or gaze at the knobs of Kentucky he so often described whilst taking in the Abbey church and Merton's final resting place in its shadow.

The Humility of Merton

After those initial moments I had the opportunity to look through the two trunks of clothing. Prior to this visit one monk who knew Merton expressed surprise that there could be two trunks of his clothing, thinking that Merton never had that many items of clothing. However, if you look through many of the photographs of Merton taken at Gethsemani over the years, he does display quite a wardrobe! (Though, having said that, the trunks also contained some bulkier items that were not clothing, such as pillows and bedding from the hermitage, as well as a heavy, over-sized Cistercian Psalter in Latin.) However, do not be deceived that Merton was receiving special treatment or, as the most famous monk in America, if not the world, he had to dress according to that part. No, no, no. And I really can't emphasize this too much. As demonstrated by his iconic jacket, Merton was allocated clothes just the same as any other monk. He didn't even blink at being issued the clothing of a deceased monk or other hand-me-downs.

Looking through the clothing in front of me much of it was frayed and worn, many items repaired numerous times, with the almost forgotten art of darning prominently displayed, almost to the point that there was more darn evident than what was left of the original clothing. Another monk who had worked in the tailors shop at the monastery, when he saw some of the repairs to the clothing, felt certain that some of the repairs had probably been undertaken by Merton himself. In contrast to the provisions laid down in his Rule by St. Benedict that a monk's habit should fit, be sufficiently warm, not too old, Merton's clothing brought to mind more the exhortation of one of the desert fathers, Abbot Pambo, who laid down that the monk's clothing should be so poor that if left on the road no one, not even a beggar, would be tempted to take it.

On occasion, some of Merton's visitors were shocked by Merton's living conditions at his Gethsemani hermitage: how bitterly cold it was in winter unless you were right beside the fireplace; having to go outside in all weathers to use an outhouse, often frequented by a snake; and the scraps of food he seemed to be eating, with no proper care for his diet, especially considering some of the severe stomach issues he faced.[1] Yet, despite his grumblings about certain things at the Abbey, the hermitage was the fulfilment of a long held sense of calling to a more solitary life and was embraced by Merton in a spirit of joy and humility, content, as St. Benedict writes in his twelve steps of humility, "with all that is mean and poor." The trunks of clothing were another, very powerful reminder of Merton's humility and self-effacing nature.

Centenary Exhibit

The timing of this donation could not have been better. The Merton Center had been working for a number of years with a local museum, the Frazier Historical Museum, on an exhibit of materials from the Merton Center archives, along with other events, to celebrate the closing of the centenary year of Merton's birth. As we were working with the Frazier a problematic issue that we encountered was that the Merton collection was almost completely a one-dimensional paper collection, with very few physical artifacts like the type that would normally be exhibited in a museum. This collection of Merton's clothing would change that quite dramatically and items from it would feature prominently in the exhibit, bringing Merton to life for visitors to the exhibit in a way that manuscripts and other documents never could.

---

[1] Edward Rice, *The Man in the Sycamore Tree: The Good Times and Hard Life of Thomas Merton.* Garden City, New York: Doubleday, 1970. p.80.

The exhibit entitled, "Thomas Merton: A Familiar Stranger," would eventually open on the last day of Merton's centennial year, January 30th, 2016 and run until the end of May. The opening reception, hosted by the Honorable Greg Fischer, Mayor of Louisville, the Most Reverend Joseph E. Kurtz, Archbishop of Louisville and President of the U.S. Conference of Bishops, and Dr. Joseph J. McGowan, President of Bellarmine University, would include a very special guest, Helen-Marie Grimes. And it is the story of Helen-Marie, and her beloved deceased husband, Robert Grimes, that you are about to read...

—Paul Pearson
November 2020

"If I have written about interracial justice, war, or thermonuclear weapons, it is because these issues are terribly relevant to one great truth: that man is called to live as a child of God. Man must respond to this call to live in peace with all his brothers and sisters in the One Christ."
—Thomas Merton

Enacting Love:

How Thomas Merton Died for Peace

The Most Famous Monk in the World

THOMAS MERTON WAS AN AMERICAN PROPHET. It has been said that he was the "Conscience of America" during the tumultuous 1960s, especially of the peace movement. He was one of the first religious figures in America to openly oppose the Vietnam War, much to the chagrin of President Lyndon Johnson, who saw the war as a test of his presidency. In 1964, Johnson told U. S. Ambassador Henry Cabot Lodge, who was Richard Nixon's vice presidential running mate against John F. Kennedy in 1960, that he didn't want to go down in history as the American president who let another Southeast Asian country fall to communism. In typical Cold War propaganda, Johnson talked about the resulting domino effect, stating that should one country fall to communism, others would fall soon thereafter.

With his friends and fellow American prophets, Martin Luther King, Jr. and Rabbi Abraham Joshua Heschel, Merton was an outspoken advocate for the nonviolent Civil Rights Movement and, lesser known, for indigenous rights. In regard to systemic racism in America, Merton wrote in a journal in July of 1961: "Race pride is revealed today as man's primary collective sin." In the entry, Merton double underlined the word "collective" for emphasis. He wrote that sincerity in righting the wrongs of America's long history of racism is insufficient: "so subjective and so ineffectual as to be worse than meaningless. It is a personal luxury, which enables the individual to feel concern—without doing anything." No doubt, if he were alive today, Merton would be dismayed that the ensuing sixty years has seen little change regarding racism in America. He would remind us that the people who say racism no longer exists in America are the very people who perpetuate it by ignoring its insidious and systemic existence.

While Merton was mostly known for the dozens of books he wrote on religion, spirituality, contemplation, and social issues, especially for his million-selling coming-to-faith autobiography, *The Seven Storey Mountain*, and other books like *Conjectures of a Guilty Bystander*, he was also an early environmentalist. For Merton, if we are to believe that God created the world, then it is our collective duty to be good stewards of God's creation, not to destroy it in the name of greed and profit. After reading Rachel Carson's *Silent Spring* in 1962, he even lent his voice to the emerging environmentalism movement in America. While the powers that be, mostly the corporations that produced pesticides and their lobbyists—tried to silence Carson and the rising influence of her popular book, Merton wrote letters to her, encouraging her to keep up the good work.

By the fall of 1968, Thomas Merton was possibly the most famous monk in the world when he left the safety and austerities of the Abbey of Our Lady of Gethsemani monastery south of Louisville, Kentucky to go on what would become known as his "Asian Journey." Along the way, he visited northern California, Alaska, and India, before his last stop in Thailand, where he attended a week-long monastic conference at a Red Cross Center outside of Bangkok. Merton could not have known at the time that he would never leave Southeast Asia alive.

Or did he?

On December 10, 1968, only two days into the conference, Merton was last seen alive as he strolled back to his bungalow after lunch, having delivered a scheduled talk during the morning session. He wanted to be alone for his noontime prayer and contemplation, called meridian. (Monks and nuns pray frequently at prescribed times throughout the day, including at noontime. Meridian is related to the sun's position in the sky at noon.) He may have simply wanted to take a nap. Either way, he planned to return to the conference to answer audience questions later in the afternoon. What transpired after that has been the subject of conjecture and conspiracy ever since. Newspaper headlines at the time reported that Merton was accidentally electrocuted by a faulty floor fan, and that heart failure may have precipitated the tragedy. The recycled stories of his accidental death took hold like a tenacious weed in the minds of a generation.

But what if his death wasn't accidental?

What if, instead, Thomas Merton was assassinated, his murder made to look like an accident?

Although Merton was loved by many, he was also despised across America for his outspoken support of civil rights, peace, nuclear disarmament, and especially for his opposition to the Cold War and the war in Vietnam, what he considered a senseless and unjust perversion of society and religion. In *Faith & Violence*, his last book published weeks before he departed on his fateful journey, Merton was especially critical of the White House administration's war mongering policies in Southeast Asia.

What has been missing from the controversy is *motive*. Why would someone want Thomas Merton dead at precisely that time? What motivated the sense of urgency behind the hasty assassination, if indeed it was assassination? Who did it? Aside from Thomas Merton and his assassin or assassins, only four other people have known the answers since 1968: Abbot Flavian and retired Abbot Fox, a fellow brother monk, and a spirited little nun who lived at a convent thirteen miles from the abbey. The secret has been safeguarded until the above-mentioned nun was the last of the four monastics still living. She was cautioned by the abbots never to reveal what she knew. Merton himself had made her promise never to reveal what he told her in the days before he left the relative safety of the abbey, where it would be difficult, if not impossible, for an impostor with malicious intent to have moved unseen among the brotherhood of monks. But in her mid-eighties and near the end of her remarkable and uncommon life, the little nun finally revealed her secret. This book describes the curious circumstances that carried her secret to your hands in the form of this book.

As with all great stories, this story begins at the beginning.

The story I am about to tell is not my story. It is the story of three people who found each other in a most unusual circumstance—unusual, that is, to most of us who can't imagine spending our lives closed off from the world in the austerity of a cloistered monastery. Although I wasn't there, my story intersects theirs, which means I also have a story to tell, an amazing tale that no one else has ever heard. I hope to tell it faithfully and credibly. I hope it moves you. I hope it changes history, at least what history will say about Thomas Merton in the future. History is fickle, often peddling lies as truths and calling truths lies. Up is down. Alternative Truths, they call it. Fake News.

America has learned that lesson the hard way, the same way she has learned that ignorance joined with power is the most ferocious enemy of truth and justice.

With that said, I should like to point out that I am certainly not the first to consider the notion that Thomas Merton may have been assassinated. James W. Douglass, theologian, peace activist and author of *JFK and the Unspeakable* (2008), the acclaimed book about Kennedy's assassination, suggested the idea during a question and answer session following his keynote speech at the 1997 International Thomas Merton Society conference in Pittsburgh. Before Douglass, Matthew Fox—a Catholic priest-turned Episcopalian priest—had spoken publicly about Merton's possible martyrdom. As a young Dominican, Fox corresponded with Merton about where he should go to earn a degree in spirituality. Merton advised him to attend the *Institut Catholique* in Paris.

I've had a number of candid phone conversations with both gentlemen. Fox told me that he felt the accidental death by faulty fan was suspicious from the very beginning. More palpably, he had spoken to a former C.I.A. agent who had been active in Southeast Asia in 1968, who replied when confronted about the possibility that Merton was assassinated by American government operatives in Bangkok, "I will neither affirm it nor deny it." Another agent said to one of Fox's students, "At that time, we in the C.I.A. in Southeast Asia were flooded with cash and with absolutely no accountability. If there was just one agent who felt Merton needed to be silenced he could have had him done away with and no questions asked." Some years later, in what amounted to a confession, a third ex-agent who was in Thailand at the time of Merton's death told Fox, "Yes, we killed Thomas Merton. And for the last forty years of my life I have been cleansing my soul for what I did as a young man working for the C.I.A. in

Southeast Asia during the Vietnam War."

In an hour-and-a-half long phone conversation on April 17, 2018, author Jim Douglass told me something disturbing he had learned first-hand from a credible witness about the cover-up of Martin Luther King, Jr.'s assassination. It involved the altering of the crime scene. Jim told me that he had related to the King family what he had learned. If true, what Jim told me could change history. But I won't go into detail. It's not my story to tell. I only have this one, as told to me by Thomas Merton's dear friend and fellow monastic, a former nun who loved her spiritual mentor and safeguarded his secret for half a century.

From the day news of Merton's death was broadcast across America, there were others like Matthew Fox who were suspicious about the circumstances of his death. I have communicated with numerous people who remember the exact moment. Emmanuel Charles McCarthy told me that he remembers sitting in a coffee shop at Notre Dame when he learned of the news. His thoughts went immediately to assassination. In the following decades, Fr. McCarthy—"Charlie" to his friends—became a prominent and respected voice on faith and nonviolence. He was the founding director of Notre Dame's Program for the Study of Nonviolent Conflict Resolution, and with Merton's friends, Dorothy Day and Gordon Zahn, McCarthy co-founded Pax Christi USA. He has been a staunch believer that, according to the teachings and examples of Jesus Christ, there is no such thing as a just war for Christians, a position that the Catholic Church has only recently begun to adopt. For his lifetime of work on faith and nonviolence, Emmanuel Charles McCarthy was nominated for the Nobel Peace Prize in 1989. I think Thomas Merton would have been proud of the priest Charlie became.

Aside from the four monastics mentioned previously, in the weeks before he left for Asia, Thomas Merton had hinted to others his somber concern that his travels abroad would be dangerous and that he might not return. In fact, in his mimeographed "Farewell Letter" to friends, Merton stated that he did not know when he would return from Asia.

Nor is there any need for me to go into the details of contradictions between official reports of Merton's death and the eye-witness accounts of individuals, all clergy, who first discovered Thomas Merton's body. In this respect, I defer to the authors of *The Martyrdom of Thomas Merton* (Turley and Martin, 2018) who laid out their argument brilliantly with supporting evidence and documentation at every step as they judiciously led readers through the transpiring events of December 10, 1968 and shortly thereafter. What is missing—and what I may offer as a complement to their achievement—is *motive* and *urgency*. Why was Thomas Merton assassinated at that very moment? What was so urgent that he had to be killed before he left the conference in Thailand? His travel itinerary indicated that he would be home in Kentucky in time for Christmas.

Some people may question why I wrote this book.

To be honest, a part of me was afraid to write it. Because of my trepidation, I put the project aside for months at a time. I regularly considered not publishing it at all. As a rule, I avoid controversy whenever possible. I'm a coward in that respect. I'm at an age where I just want peace in my life. I don't put much stock in conspiracy theories, either. No ancient aliens who built the pyramids or created the giant geoglyphs, known as the Nasca Lines in the high desert of southern Peru, for me. It would have been easier and safer for me to let sleeping dogs lie. What is done is done. So why take the risk? Why chance contempt? Why rattle history's cage? I kept asking myself will anyone even care about what I have to say. And I knew for whatever reasons, some people will not believe the story I am about to tell. They will try to find fault with every little thing in an attempt to demean the significance of this book or to preserve their naïve belief that America never does wrong.

That is on them.

My concern was so great at times that I feared for my own safety. Some secrets must never be revealed, no matter how much time has passed. I worried about reprisal. I worried so much, in fact, that several close friends have sealed letters to be opened in the event of my death, whether reported as accidental or not . . . a busted brake line while going down a steep and narrow road, poisoned underwear, or a plugged-in hair dryer falling into a relaxing bubble bath, if you get my gist.

But the story persisted. The truth wanted out.

For the longest time the working title of this book was *Finding Thomas Merton*. But as time went by and the arc of the manuscript began to take shape, I realized that the book would be much more than just a retelling of my discovery of Thomas Merton's worldly possessions. The importance of the book slowly became apparent. To be honest, I had not known much about Thomas Merton before. I didn't know what questions to ask, so I listened a good deal and took copious notes. But the more I learned from my research and interviews, the more I realized the significance of what Helen Marie told me.

From reading many of the books that Thomas Merton wrote and was reading in the 1960s, I came to understand that everything in his life was leading him to Asia, even though the journey might ultimately spell his demise. Merton was learning that to be a Follower of Christ—as any good priest or monk must be—he had to do more than he had been doing from the safety of the monastery. He had to do more than just to pray for a better world, a Heaven on Earth. He needed to put actions of compassion and justice into practice. He needed to enact love. He needed to be a force for peace. Merton was mindful of the obligation in the Bible to "love justice and to seek it out" (Amos 5:15). As the assassination of his friend Martin Luther King, Jr. only months earlier had taught him, sometimes doing the right thing can be costly.

It is a curious fact that both Merton and King died within months of each other in the same year that also saw the assassination of Robert Kennedy, who is directly connected to Merton's story through his wife, Ethel, with whom Merton corresponded in an effort to better understand Bobby's and President Kennedy's views on nuclear armament, the Cold War, and civil rights.

1968 was a terrible year in that respect.

But what if there was a third assassination that year? What if Thomas Merton was also assassinated?

In writing this book, I was mindful of something Martin Luther King, Jr. once famously said: "The arc of history is long, but it bends towards justice." I wanted to help bend the arc of what history has said about the death of Thomas Merton for more than half a century. I wanted the world to know why he had risked his life for the love of others. I wanted to bring about some justice for the man who was so much better than I will ever be.

For the sake of history's arc and for justice, I felt compelled to write this book. After all, if Thomas Merton was assassinated, then he died a martyr, and he deserves to be declared as such so that his name can join that revered litany of men and women throughout history who gave their lives in defense of their faith or in order to save others. As John 15:13 says, "There is no greater love than to lay down one's life for [others]." Knowing what I now knew, I wrote to Pope Francis requesting that he declare Thomas Merton a martyr. In the case of Thomas Merton, this book will show that he gave up his life willingly to save tens of thousands of lives—American and Vietnamese—by attempting to bring about an expeditious end to the Vietnam War. He would surrender his life for the lives of people he had never met. He would be a peacemaker, as Jesus instructed all his followers to be.

The three main characters in this book went by different names at different times—such is tradition when men and women become monks and priests and nuns. Even newly elected popes take on new names. It is especially true for those who live in cloistered monasteries or convents. After taking his Trappist vows at the Abbey of Our Lady of Gethsemani in Kentucky, Thomas Merton was henceforth known to other religious and to those close to him as Father Louis, affectionately pronounced Father Loo-ee. Some friends referred to him simply as "Louie." He also went by Brother Monk (br. M.). Some friends called him Tom. Some still do. To further complicate things, the abbots mentioned in this book went by Abbot, Father, Father Monk, and even Brother Monk. The monastery abbot is sometimes called Dom (e.g. Dom Flavian). The nun, who is so central to this story, went by Helen Marie before taking her religious vows, and as Sister Mary Pius thereafter, only to return to Helen Marie after dispensation released her from her religious order shortly after Merton's death. Because this book spans periods of time before, during, and after life as a monastic, the proper noun usage can be a bit confusing at times. Throughout this book, the author has judiciously done his best to avoid confusion.

He apologizes in advance where he has failed.

This book took six years for me to write. For someone who has written an average of two or three books a year for decades, that's saying something about the carefulness and significance of this project. Of the books I have written so far, this was by far the most difficult to write. The problem was in trying to weave the disparate threads of the book together in some logical and compelling order. At times, I almost gave up on it entirely. But I made a promise to Thomas Merton's nun friend that I would tell her story. I made the same promise to Thomas Merton.

I intended to keep my promise.

Finally, a good friend pointed out that unlike the historian who digs through documents in musty libraries and has no personal part in the history itself, the author of this book was part of the story. He was there. He interacted with some of the characters in this book. It was his "discovery" (for lack of a better word) of certain artifacts or relics that prompted the arc of this story in the first place. As such, the author's voice sometimes intrudes on the telling in ways not usually found in history books or nonfiction. At times, the lines are blurred. He is the detached narrator here; he is a character in the story there.

The author apologizes for these unavoidable intrusions as well.

The Assassination of Thomas Merton

On December 10, 1968, while America was still reeling from the assassinations of Martin Luther King, Jr. and Bobby Kennedy, a light snow fell quietly on the Abbey of Our Lady of Gethsemani, the Trappist monastery near Bardstown, Kentucky where Dr. King's priest friend, Thomas Merton, had lived, worked, written, and prayed for twenty-seven years. Founded in 1848 and named for the Virgin Mary, Gethsemani is the oldest monastery in the United States.

By afternoon, the snow, which had briefly turned the hills and knobs white, turned to rain.

The weather was very different in Bangkok, Thailand, where Merton was attending a week-long interreligious conference from December 8th to the 15th that was organized in large part so that Southeast Asian Catholic monastics could meet Merton and listen to his lectures. In recent years, Merton had studied and written a great deal about Zen Buddhism, and he advocated for better East-West religious dialog and relations in accordance with the Second Vatican Council's (Vatican II's) commitment to better interreligious relations and religious tolerance, especially in the wake of the atrocities of World War II and the Holocaust.

The conference was scheduled during the last leg of what later became known as Merton's Asian Journey. In the weeks before the conference, which was held at the Red Cross Center about thirty miles from downtown Bangkok, Merton had met with His Holiness the Dalai Lama at his mountain residence in Dharmsala, northern India. The Dalai Lama later stated that he believed Merton had a deeper understanding of Buddhism than any other Christian he had ever met. According to his itinerary, Merton would return to the United States directly after the conference. The two-month trip was Merton's first prolonged leave from the monastery in almost three decades, aside from brief hospitalizations, the most recent for debilitating back pain in the spring of 1966. At that rate, it would probably be his last. At fifty-three, Merton planned to spend the rest of his life living in his simple hermitage in the woods where he would continue to read, write, pray, and take long contemplative walks through the surrounding monastery grounds, which at 2,000 acres, were substantial. After all, Trappists are members of the Order of Cistercians of the Strict Observance (O.C.S.O.). Even getting permission from the abbot to build his little cinderblock cabin in the woods was historic. Merton was the rare American Trappist monk permitted to live away from the monastery and the rest of his brother monks.

It took him a while to adjust to his newfound isolation.

On his way to Asia, Merton spent a week in Eagle River, a small bedroom community about a dozen miles north of Anchorage, where he gave a series of talks as part of a religious conference. His Alaskan visit caused some to speculate that he was searching for a location to build a new Trappist monastery or, perhaps, a new hermitage for himself, one even more remote and inaccessible to the ever-growing intrusions of outside life. It seemed as though people were always dropping in to visit him, including singer Joan Baez and our mutual friend, the poet Denise Levertov. He may have also been concerned for his safety. In the wake of his protests against racism and the war in Vietnam, Merton had encountered strange men waiting to waylay him along the dirt road up to his hermitage. He stayed hidden in the woods to circumvent their nefarious plans. He wrote about it in his letters, but according to Br. Irenaeus, he also asked his brother monks to be vigilant of strangers in their midst who might be out to harm him. Despite the speculation by scholars, Helen Marie told me that, before he left, Thomas Merton had told her that he was not looking for a place to build a new hermitage for himself.

On the morning of December 10, 1968, Merton delivered his much-anticipated lecture. And this lecture was filmed. His speech was well applauded, but without rousing cheers. Conference attendees may have expected a talk on the interior life of spiritualism—the power of prayer, meditation, and contemplation. Or perhaps they expected him to talk about the life of a Trappist monk, or about the duty of religious to seek justice and peace and to relieve suffering, which tied into his activism in the Civil Rights Movement and anti-war protests. Maybe they wanted to hear his thoughts on the similarities between Christianity and Buddhism in light of his recent travels and experiences, and his meeting with the Dalai Lama. But his title was "Marxism and Monastic Perspectives." Fr. Matthew Fox recently reminded me that, during the height of the Cold War, any lecture with the word "Marxism" in the title was bound to draw the attention of the C.I.A.

After his morning talk and lunch, Merton returned to his bungalow for a break as the conference wasn't scheduled to begin again until several hours later in the day. The way I heard it, one of the fellow priests, Fr. Celestine Say, from the Philippines, saw that Merton left accompanied by Reverend François De Grunne, a priest from Belgium.

In the months before he left on his Asian Journey, Thomas Merton was increasingly convinced that the government had been intercepting his mail, both coming and going. Like his friends Martin Luther King, Jr. and Daniel and Philip Berrigan, Merton had become a real thorn in the side of President Johnson and his administration for his role in stirring the flames of the Civil Rights Movement and anti-war protests across America. Hadn't his friend Martin Luther King, Jr. been silenced forever only a few months earlier?

In his eulogy for his late friend, U. S. Congressman John Lewis, former President Bill Clinton related something that Lewis had once told him. During the Civil Rights march from Selma to Montgomery on March 7, 1965, a then-young John Lewis in a tan overcoat wore a backpack which contained only a few items: an orange, an apple, his toothbrush (he was certain he'd be arrested and spend a few days in jail. Lewis was arrested for protesting more than fifty times in his life, five times while as a sitting U.S. Congressman), and a book: Thomas Merton's *The Seven Storey Mountain* (see photo below).

As more than 500 protesters marched peacefully across the Edmund Pettus Bridge, armed policemen savagely beat them with billy-clubs while a horrified America watched news footage on their televisions. Lewis' skull was cracked open from a blow. The infamous day is remembered as "Bloody Sunday." Photos from that tragic day clearly show Lewis wearing his backpack. Like Merton, John Lewis passionately embraced Jesus's admonishment that "actions speak louder than words." As a Black man, Lewis saw the parallel in the old African American proverb, "When you pray, move your feet."

From the examples of Jesus and Thomas Merton, Lewis expounded the notion of "making good and necessary trouble" when it comes to peacefully resolving social justice issues. During his long tenure in Congress, Lewis was hailed as the "Conscience of Congress." More than ever, that worthy house could use more men and women like John Lewis.

(John Lewis, right, with backpack)

In his "Cold War Letters," Merton had prophesied the assassination of President John F. Kennedy for his peace-making policies, in opposition to his war-mongering military and C.I.A. advisors who pushed for a preemptive nuclear strike on the Soviet Union. If Merton's letters had indeed been intercepted by the government, then they knew his travel itinerary. They knew exactly when and where he would be in Thailand, the final leg of his Asian Journey before he would return home to the relative safety of the monastery, where it would be virtually impossible for agents to infiltrate the close-knit, cloistered community of the monastery wherein everyone had known each other for years, decades even. In the busy, crowded streets of Bangkok, agents could hide among the millions of unfamiliar people milling about during wartime.

In fact, on the day before his death, Merton returned to his bungalow and found the door was unlocked. He was certain he had locked it when he left. When he went inside, he saw that things in his room had been rearranged or moved. This isn't speculation. Merton reported the incident to another monk at the time. This point bears repeating: *The day before Thomas Merton was found dead, he was certain that someone had gone into his locked room and messed with his things.*

On the day he died, Merton returned to his bungalow after his morning lecture and lunch for his meridian. He had been too busy the day before to observe it. As stated previously, a Belgian priest named François de Grunne was seen accompanying Merton to his bungalow. De Grunne's room was on the second floor directly above Fr. Celestine Say's. Merton's room was separated from Say's on the first floor by a small parlor. Rather than walls, the room had makeshift partitions. Occupants could hear everything in the other room and see in if they chose to look. Only a few minutes after Say's arrival, while he was brushing his teeth, de Grunne came to the bathroom door and asked if Fr. Say had heard a shout. Say reported that he had heard nothing. It would have been an easy matter for either of them to look into Merton's room at that point to check on him, but neither did. De Grunne simply returned to his room. Say never heard any sound from Merton's room from the moment of his arrival until the discovery of Merton's body.

When Merton was found dead two hours after he had returned to his bungalow, he was lying on the floor with his hands at his side. A stand fan was lying across his body at the hip and the fan was still running. Merton's skin was burned where the fan rested on his exposed skin. A German Benedictine nun, who was also a doctor, from a monastery in Korea, was one of the first witnesses to reach Merton's body. Purportedly, she tried to resuscitate Merton at first, but quickly declared that he was dead. She observed a bleeding wound on the back of Merton's head. From the first days after Merton's death, the

Thai newspapers said the cause of his death was heart failure (not to be confused with a heart attack) while the American press reported that Merton died from accidental electrocution.

The day after Merton's death, a letter by six Trappist delegates present at the Bangkok conference was wired to the Abbot of Gethsemani to report what they knew of Merton's death and to express their condolences. Below is an excerpt of the letter reproduced precisely as it was typed. A mimeograph of the original letter was given to Brother Irenaeus and other monks by Abbot (Dom) Flavian with an accompanying letter dated December 19, 1968 reporting on "the sudden death of our Father Louis Merton," and was part of the artifacts stowed in the trunks for almost fifty years.

Sawang Kaniwat, Bangkok
11 December 1968

Dear Dom Flavian,

The news of the sudden and unexpected death of your beloved son, Father Louis, has already been conveyed to you. However, we the undersigned, as the Trappist delegates to this historic Conference, wish to convey to you, and through you to all our brethren at Gethsemani, the information that we know you would be anxious to know . . .

[Skipping four brief paragraphs]

On the morning of his [Merton's] death he had delivered to us the paper that he had prepared and all were eagerly looking forward to the evening session when he was to answer questions on his paper and on matters dealing with monasticism in general.

After lunch he retired to his room and on the way commented

to one of us that he was looking forward to his meridian as he
had been unable to have it the day before due to an organiz-
ing meeting that he had to attend.

Not long after he retired a shout was heard by others in his
cottage but after a preliminary check they thought they must
have imagined the cry.

He was found at the end of the meridian and when found was
lying on the floor in his pajamas. He was on his back with the
electric fan lying across his chest. The fan was still switched
on and there was a deep burn and some cuts on his right side
and arm. The back of his head was bleeding slightly.

One of the nuns who had medical experience was quickly at
his side but it was evident that he was already dead.

A Thai doctor came and later another Thai doctor arrived. It
is difficult to determine at this stage just exactly what was the
cause of his death.

It is believed that he could have showered and then had a
heart attack near the fan, and in falling knocked the fan over
against himself; or again that being in his bare feet on a stone
floor he may have received a fatal shock.

As soon as the police had finished their investigation we asked
permission to dress the body in his robe and scapular and this
permission they readily gave.

The body was then toweled and then dressed and laid out on
his bed. We then kept a constant vigil beside his body . . .

In death Father Louis' face was set in a great and deep peace
and it was obvious that he had found Him Whom he had
searched for so diligently.

> The American Army took his body to their hospital in Bangkok
> . . .
>
> [skipping two paragraphs]
>
> Again extending to you and all our brothers at Gethsemani our heartfelt sympathy and an assurance of a continued remembrance of Father Louis in our Masses and prayers that his soul may rest in peace.
>
> > Your brothers and sisters in Christ,
> > (Signed by the six Trappist delegates at the conference)
> > Dom Anselm Parker, O.C.S.O., Australia
> > Dom Joachim Murphy, O.C.S.O., New Zealand
> > Dom Simeon Chang, O.C.S.O., Hong Kong
> > Mother Christiana, O.C.S.O., Japan
> > Dom M. F. Acharya, O.C.S.O., India
> > Dom M. Frans Hardjawijata, O.C.S.O., Indonesia

It is worth noting that although the letter begins with "we the undersigned" and concludes with "Signed by the six Trappist delegates," the mimeographed letter includes no signatures. In fact, the letter as it appears above is not the original letter that was wired to the Abbey by the six delegates, but a facsimile. Abbot Flavian himself tells us so. In a letter on Abbey of Gethsemani stationery dated December 19, 1968, he wrote: "Dear Friends . . . Since many of you have requested more information regarding the details of his [Merton's] death, we are reproducing here the letter we received from the six Trappist-Cistercian Superiors who were there with him at the meeting in Bangkok."

Dr. Paul Pearson suggested that the statement about Merton having showered was likely not included in the original and was added by someone who had been close to Merton in attempt to "make some sense" of the events that led up to his death. When I specifically asked Pearson if he knew the whereabouts of the original (signed) letter, he responded that he had never seen it and that "perhaps it ended up in the archives at Gethsemani amongst Abbatial papers. Though, having said that, Abbot Flavian, from what I've heard, wasn't a great one for preserving things" (Personal Communication, March 24, 2021).

Pearson was certain that the letter was reproduced in the immediate aftermath of Merton's death. It is likely that a fellow monk typed the facsimile at the request of Abbot Flavian to accompany his letter of December 19, 1968. One possible explanation for the facsimile may be that the original letter, which had been wired from Bangkok on the 11th, was not legibly reproducible on the mimeograph machine. Telegrams from Western Union were often printed in tele-type font on yellow paper, which may have affected the ability of the mimeograph machine to make legible copies. Therefore, in order to print sufficient readable copies of the letter for monks and others "Friends," it had to be typed anew on plain white paper. I, for one, can attest to the notoriously poor quality of mimeograph reproductions. In high school during the late 1970s—only ten years after Merton's death—I was a student helper in the main office. I was frequently asked to make mimeographs for teachers.

When the Thai police were done with their cursory investigation, Merton's body was sent to a U.S. Army hospital in Bangkok where no autopsy was done. He was only 53 years old, was height-to-weight proportionate (stocky, but not overweight), generally healthy (despite chronic stomach issues; see comment in Paul Pearson's foreword), took long, contemplative walks daily, and had lived for decades a monk's austere existence—which included manual labor—and existed on a simple diet without red meat or alcohol. Yet the official cause of death was listed as "sudden heart failure." The Thai Police report made no mention of the bleeding head wound on the back of Merton's head. *What caused it? How deep was the injury?* The report simply asserted that Thomas Merton suffered heart failure and collapsed, pulling down a fan with him which, by a quirk of fate, had a faulty wire that electrocuted him (although the maids who regularly cleaned the room were never shocked, nor had previous tenants of the room been shocked).

History would report that unspectacular death for the next half century—precisely as his assassin(s) had planned. No one would be the wiser. One of America's most outspoken critics against oppression, bigotry, violence, and war—the "Conscience of America" during the peace movement—was forever silenced by a fan. Five days after his death, Merton's body was returned to the United States in a military transport plane. Ironically, the body of the man who had spent years protesting the war was returned to America along with the corpses of young American soldiers also killed in Southeast Asia. A dated cargo receipt shows that Merton's personal effects (his luggage) were returned to Kentucky via a Pan American flight almost a month later on January 16, 1969.

Merton died twenty-seven years to the day after he first arrived at The Abbey of Our Lady of Gethsemani (he did not enter the monastery as a postulant until December 13, the feast of St. Lucy. For three days, he stayed in the guest house where Helen Marie would stay a quarter century later). In almost prophesy of his future demise, the last line of *The Seven Storey Mountain*, published in 1947, twenty-one years before he died, seems to presage Merton's death by electrocution and the subsequent burning of his flesh. In the passage, God who is speaking to Merton says:

And when you have been praised a little and loved a lit-

tle I will take away all your gifts and all your love and all
your praise and you will be utterly forgotten and aban-
doned and you will be nothing, a rejection. And in that
day you shall begin to possess the solitude you have so
long desired. And your solitude will bear immense fruit in
the souls of men you will never see on earth.

Do not ask when it will be or where or how it will be. On
a mountain or in a prison, in a desert or in a concentration camp or in a hospital or at Gethsemani. It does not
matter. So do not ask me, because I am not going to tell
you. You will not know until you are in it.

But you shall taste the true solitude of my anguish and my
poverty and I shall lead you into the high places of my joy
and you shall die in Me and find all things in My mercy
which has created you for this end and brought you from
Prades to Bermuda to St. Antonin to Oakham to London
to Cambridge to Rome to New York to Columbia to Cor-
pus Christi to St. Bonaventure to the Cistercian Abbey of
the poor men who labor at Gethsemani:

That you may become the brother of God and learn to
know the Christ of the burnt men. (462)

I have always taken that last line of the book to mean that Thomas
Merton and others like him—his brother monks and brother priests—
had been burnt by the consuming love of God, by the flame of love
of which St. John of the Cross spoke, and by the divine spark of love
that should be kindled in the hearts of all humanity.

The question is not are the events portrayed above *true*, but
whether they are *credible*. Sometimes in murder there is no smoking gun, especially in a case as cold as this one. To this question and

its profound ramifications if proven true, I can only give the reply of one destitute man's opinion. My connections to this story—what Merton called "relationships"—are unique and cast an intriguing perspective that no other individual could bring to bear on this story. This is not ego or bravado talking. It is not an effort at unabashed sensationalism in order to sell books. As I said from the beginning, I never had any intention to write a book about Thomas Merton. I did so only because a sweet and kind former nun who was Thomas Merton's student and friend asked me to tell her story, and she had the resolve to endure years of interviews with me.

It is my estimation that the preponderance of evidence presented in the following pages—circumstantial and otherwise—will reveal the *likelihood* that assassination is precisely what happened to Thomas Merton that fateful day on the outskirts of Bangkok. The details reported about his death aren't the crucial ones: whether or not he had showered; or whether he first had a heart attack and then collapsed onto the faulty fan. Recent books like *The Martyrdom of Thomas Merton* (Turley and Martin, 2018) demonstrate that I am not alone in my conjecture that Thomas Merton was assassinated.

But they were not the first.

The story revealed in the following pages will complement those earlier brave voices and may, at times, lean on them for support. In the end, what matters is that the truth of what happened to Thomas Merton becomes history and that his legacy be regarded for what it is: a poor man bereft of anything but his eloquent words and his enormous love, who, in life, gave his all to help diminish suffering, racial prejudice, religious intolerance, and the horrors of war; a man who gave his life that in doing so he might save others, for as a Christian, the Bible charged him that there is no greater action than to give one's life to save others (John 15:13). As a faithful priest, Merton was compelled to heed Jesus's instruction to be a peacemaker (Matthew 5:9). While writers like Hugh Turley and David Martin have delineated the conspiracy, what they have not been able to identify clearly is *motive*. Why was Thomas Merton assassinated when he was? What was the crucial thing that had to be stopped at that exact time? Why not wait until he returned to Kentucky?

I hope this book can answer that question.

For years, as I wrote this book, I prayed that I tell this story true so that the individual(s) who assassinated Thomas Merton would not get away with murder.

The Monk Who Fell From the Sky

As I said at the beginning, there are three main characters in this story: Thomas Merton, of course; the nun who was Merton's friend and mentee; and a fellow brother monk whose story of how he ended up at the Abbey of Gethsemani is not unlike the story of many of the disillusioned young men who entered the monastery after WWII.

The following narrative was transcribed and adapted from journals, notes, articles, official records, and photographs about Robert Grimes (formerly Sergeant Grimes, U. S. Air Corps, 1939-1945) made available to me by his widow for my research.

Like many young men looking for adventure and the chance to prove themselves during World War II, Robert "Bobby" Grimes was only fifteen years old when he ran away from home and enlisted in the Army in late 1939. At five foot three inches tall and one hundred twenty pounds, he looked more thirteen than fifteen. He wasn't fooling anyone, especially the Army doctor who gave him a physical examination to determine his fitness for service. Although the Army allowed him to sign up, the recruiter told him that his parents had to send a letter attesting that he was at least seventeen years of age. In his ensuing letter home, Robert asked his parents to tell the Army that he was born in 1921. He ended his letter with the threat that his parents would never see him again if they didn't help him by lying to the U. S. government. Fearful of losing their son forever, his parents complied.

(Fifteen year old private Robert "Bobby" Grimes after completing Basic Training, c. 1940)

By June of 1942, with American participation in the war in its sixth month, Robert was still stateside. He was missing all the action he heard about on the radio and saw in newsreels. He asked to transfer to the Air Corps, then a branch of the Army, despite being warned by his commanding officer that the life expectancy in air combat was something like three minutes. Oddly, the warning only fueled Robert's determination to transfer. He wanted to be in the thick of it, not sitting around in the states marching and drilling and peeling potatoes during KP. Flying was considered hazardous duty. Therefore, service was strictly voluntary, which meant that airmen had it pretty good.

In May of 1943, after more than ten months of flying and gunnery training, Robert was shipped overseas. He thought he was being sent to the Pacific Theater, and in fact, had mosquito netting and his jungle kit stowed in his pack. But even as the engines were revving before takeoff, new orders came over the radio. They were being routed to England instead. Robert was glad on hearing the news. He had hoped to go to England. Hours later, after crossing the Atlantic, Robert landed at Grafton-Underwood, home of the 384th Bombardment Group (Heavy), 545th Bombardment Squadron of the 8th Air Force. The base would later have the distinction of being the base from which the first and last bomb raids were launched over Germany in World War II.

("A Gunner's Day Off," England 1943. Robert second from right)

At Grafton-Underwood, Robert joined the crew of a B-17 Flying Fortress. It was a custom back then to name the aircraft or to paint some picture on the fuselage near the nose to identify the plane. On Robert's B-17 was painted in large white letters, "We Dood It" from a line in comedian Red Skelton's radio show. As the smallest crewmember, Robert was assigned to the dual .50-caliber tail guns, which would be a tight squeeze for anyone much larger. The 10-man crew was comprised of the pilot, co-pilot, navigator, bombardier, ball turret gunner, a radioman/gunner, two waist gunners, and an engineer/top gunner. All but the six gunners were officers. Robert eventually made sergeant.

(Sergeant Grimes, center)

His first mission was in June 1943. It was a daylight bombing raid on Nazi-held Antwerp, Belgium. The Allies needed the port city. Forty bombers left that morning escorted by British Spitfires that stayed with the bombers only as far as halfway across France before returning to base. Half the mission would be without fighter escort. The Germans figured that out pretty fast. They'd wait until the Spitfires left and then they'd attack. The gunners were instructed to shoot at any unknown plane with less than four engines that pointed its nose at them. It's almost impossible to tell friend or foe from a nose-on approach. In the fog of war, a few Spitfires had been shot down accidentally when they came at a formation of B-17s and were shot down by their allies. The British used to say, "We lost more good men to American gunners than we did to Germans."

Robert never forgot his first experience in aerial combat—the German Messerschmitts swooping gracefully down on them like birds of prey, guns flashing, and the white explosions of flak dotting the sky like bursting flowers. In a strange way it was almost beautiful if not surreal. The whole scene looked like something out of a movie. Although he knew the German fighters were firing real bullets, and he knew how thin the metal skin was on the B-17, Robert never felt afraid. He was too caught up in the dreamlike nature of the scene to be afraid. When the attack was over and the Messerschmitts had peeled off and headed back to their home base, Robert realized that he had never fired his guns. He had been too fascinated by the whole thing. He was embarrassed until he learned that one of the waist gunners had never fired his guns either.

Robert never did develop a healthy sense of fear of the Luftwaffe fighters. He felt that shooting them down was like a shooting gallery, the kind at a fair. It just seemed too easy. Yet, in his seven months of aerial combat, he never put in a claim for downing an enemy fighter. Honest as he was, there were just too many gunners shooting at the same airplane to say you were the one who shot it down. What did unsettle him was anti-aircraft flak, which appeared suddenly and filled the sky, the explosions like a giant invisible hand that grabbed the bomber and shook it and slammed it down.

One thing Robert remembered well about aerial combat was the quiet. With the roar of the B-17's four engines and the muffled headsets they wore to communicate, combat was not the way it is depicted in the movies: no shrill sound of the diving fighters, no sound of their machine guns firing. Even his own twin .50 calibers seemed oddly quiet.

The second half of 1943 was a bad one for U. S. airmen. Nearly a third of them were shot down before they completed their 25th and final mission. On August 17, 1943, 230 B-17s bombed the ball bearing factory at Schweinfurt, Germany. The factory was vital to Germany's war effort, providing some seventy percent of all ball bearings to Germany's aircraft industry. After the raid, the production was cut in half. However, the bomb raid came at a price. Some sixty B-17s were shot down, compared to only twenty-five German fighters. That's six hundred allied lives lost compared to twenty-five Nazis. Out of ten bombers in the squadron that left Grafton-Underwood, Robert's bomber was the only one that returned home.

A second raid on the Schweinfurt factory on October 14th disrupted production of ball bearings for six weeks, substantially slowing down Germany's ability to produce aircraft to counter the number the Allies were able to put into the air. But that raid also saw the loss of another sixty bombers, another six hundred souls lost. Robert recognized the German fighters that attacked them on both raids. They were from the "Yellow Nose Squadron," also called "Goering's Circus," for the way the pilots painted their planes' noses and landing gear bright red and yellow.

Combat on both raids was fierce. The Germans could not allow the bombers to reach Schweinfurt. At times, the fighters came in so close that the gunners had to be sure not to shoot their own planes. But sometimes it happened nonetheless. One time, a spent .50 caliber brass shell casing fell into the propeller of a B-17 flying in formation below it, and the propeller shredded the shell into shrapnel, which tore through the cockpit and killed the pilot as sure as if he had been shot. During the attacks, B-17s seemed to fall out of the sky right and left, from above and below, which was the most heartbreaking sight of all. Robert watched in horror as the smoke-billowing bombers fell into a spiral nose-dive toward the earth, the centrifugal force of the spin preventing the crew from parachuting out. He knew his number could be up at any time just as theirs had.

One of Robert's fellow crew members was a nineteen year old from Bloomington, Illinois named Billy. They say men in combat make fast friends, a band of brothers, and all that. Billy and Robert and the other non-commissioned officers on his crew spent a good deal of their down time together. They even explored parts of England together on furloughs. Billy was the ball turret gunner. The ball turret was a mostly glass sphere that jutted from the belly of the airplane. The gunner slid down into the cramped sphere, strapped himself in, and, using foot pedals, could swivel the turret left or right while firing his machine guns at enemy fighters coming at the bomber from below. (Imagine the laser guns on the Millennial Falcon in the original *Star Wars*.) It was a miserable and dangerous job. If the hydraulics failed and the landing wheels could not be lowered, the pilot would do a controlled crash landing on the plane's belly, crushing the unfortunate gunner instantly.

Close to Schweinfurt, the stream of bullets from one of the swarming bright red and yellow German fighters hit the ball turret. Later, when the "We Dood It" returned to base, the turret had been shot up so bad that there was nothing left of Billy. Years later, Robert would read Randall Jarrell's short poem about World War II, "The Death of the Ball Turret Gunner" (1945), with its haunting last lines:

> Six miles from earth, loosed from its dream of life,
> I woke to black flak and the nightmare fighters.
> When I died they washed me out of the turret with a hose.

To Robert, the poem was spot on. He would never be able to read the poem without conjuring the ghastly image of what happened to his friend Billy.

Somewhere over Norway, October, 1943, Robert, now nineteen years old, scanned the ground from the tail of the B-17, looking for targets a few hundred feet below. For a crew of a Flying Fortress, it was rare to be so close to the ground. Usually, they bombed from about 30,000 feet, more than five miles above the earth. But on some missions into occupied territory, they didn't release their bomb loads unless they could see a target.

On this day, they had come in low to get beneath cloud cover. They were informed that their target was an aluminum plant, but in reality they would be dropping their ordnance, about 6,000 pounds per plane, on a heavy water plant. Back then, no one in any of the bombers had any idea what atomic fission was or understood the importance of heavy water in the development of an atomic weapon.

As a tail gunner, Robert wasn't concerned with the aluminum plant; that was the bombardier's job. Instead, he was watching the ground looking for targets he could strafe with his dual .50 caliber guns: German staff cars, trains, even people. The Norwegians had been warned of the raid in advance, so most likely anyone out in the open was German.

(Robert wearing his leather bomber's jacket, c. 1943)

In December of 1943, the U.S. 8th Air Force and Britain's Royal Air Force (RAF) combined to bomb the German city of Hamburg for seven consecutive days and nights. The RAF did the night saturation bombing while the U.S. did precision bombing during the day. The main targets were the city's port and submarine pens, but, as was often the case, most of the city was destroyed in the process, and thousands of civilians were incinerated in the ensuing firestorms.

Robert's B-17 was in formation, headed to Hamburg, when one of the engines started acting up. Over the shipboard intercom, the pilot informed the crew that he was only getting about half power from the engine. He asked for a vote: do they continue the mission, or do they return to base to fix the engine? The crew voted to stay the course. However, they encountered heavy flak over Germany, which knocked out two of their engines. They had no choice but to turn back and try to limp home on one good engine and one that delivered only about half power. Fortunately, several U.S. P-51 "Mustangs" peeled off and escorted the crippled bomber back toward the North Sea, where German pilots gave up pursuit. The Mustangs banked and turned back toward the formation. Suddenly, the struggling bomber was alone over the cold, gray sea. Not long after that, the engine that was acting up coughed, sputtered, and died. They were staying aloft on a single engine. Despite the stall warning light and accompanying buzzing sound, their airspeed was just enough to keep them airborne. The pilot ordered the crew to jettison everything they could to lighten the load. The 6,000 pounds of bombs went first, followed by the guns and ammunition. The crippled bomber was a sitting duck for any fighter they might encounter. But that worried the crew less than the likelihood that they'd have to ditch the plane in the sea if the one good engine failed. The plane flew so low that spray from the sea was freezing onto the ship's metal surfaces.

The co-pilot came back from the cockpit with a candy bar in his hand and coolly told the men that it looked like they were going to have to ditch the plane. He told them to get ready. Robert thought about the frigid water below.

By luck or by miracle, the plane managed to climb back up to 3,000 feet (maybe a strong head wind gave it some lift). They landed at Grafton-Underwood forty-five minutes behind the rest of the bombers returning home after completing their mission. By then, the other airmen were already divvying up their belongings, which was standard practice when a plane didn't return from a mission. They learned later that the RAF had been monitoring their progress by radar and had ordered a ship to intercept their flight path just in case they had gone into the drink.

As the war continued, Germany became desperate to protect its new territories and the Fatherland. The war in the sky was as vicious and deadly as the war on the ground and the sea. By the end, the Allies would lose some 160,000 airmen and almost 34,000 aircraft over Europe. For the Third Reich, more than half a million civilians were killed in bomb raids, including as many as 100,000 in a single terrible night in Dresden on February 13, 1945.

On January 20, 1944, the base chaplain blessed the crew of the "We Dood It" as they kneeled on the tarmac in front of the aircraft before a mission while someone snapped a photo. Little could they have known that it would be the last photograph ever taken of the plane and its crew.

(B-17 Flying Fortress "We Dood It" at Grafton-Underwood; Robert Grimes kneeling second from right while the base chaplain blesses the crew)

Ten days after the photograph was taken, on January 30, 1944, Robert was sent out in his 25th mission. Army Air Corp policy back then was that if you were lucky enough to have survived twenty-five missions, you earned the right to be shipped stateside to teach new recruits. Because more than a third of all bombers were shot down, it would be demoralizing to be sent back up endlessly, each mission significantly increasing the probability that your ticket would be punched. It would be tantamount to suicide. Knowing there was an end-game for every airman gave some solace. Knowing beforehand that this was to be his last mission, Robert had already packed his bags to go home.

Somewhere over Germany on the way to Brunswick, Robert was blazing away at the swooping enemy Junkers when the B-17 suddenly shuddered like a blind-sided boxer. The intercom immediately went dead, and when he looked around he saw the right wing was on fire. Several things went through the nineteen year old's mind, not the least of which was that he'd better get out of there if the plane was going down. But considering that they were over Nazi Germany, he didn't want to jump too soon, especially if there was a chance the pilot could coax the wounded plane back to England.

Robert decided to stay at his guns, at least for a while, and sent a burst of machine gun fire at another fighter as it dove through the formation of bombers, spread out above and below him as far as the eye could see. They were at about 30,000 feet and the earth below them was hidden by a solid ceiling of clouds.

Soon, however, he noticed the flames spreading along the wing and the plane began to wobble alarmingly, which is usually an indication that the pilot is dead or seriously wounded. He decided to find out what was happening, so he squeezed through the claustrophobic passageway toward the cockpit. Midway, he discovered a large ragged hole in the fuselage, apparently the result of a direct hit by a rocket fired from one of the Junkers. Both mid-gunners, called "waist gunners," were dead, lying in a pool of blood. The radio operator was also dead, slumped over like a marionette with its strings cut. He feared that the pilot and co-pilot were dead as well.

Realizing that there were still a dozen five hundred pound bombs and thousands of gallons of fuel still onboard, which could ignite and explode at any minute, Robert decided it was time to bail out. He knew if he waited until the plane went down in a spin it would be too late. But in the excitement, he forgot his oxygen mask and he was beginning to feel the dizzying effects of oxygen deprivation. When the plane lurched again, he was thrown to the floor and covered in the blood of his two dead comrades. Robert managed to pull himself to the open doorway where he looked out into the bright, cold, roaring sky.

He took a deep breath, as if he were about to plunge into a swimming pool, and jumped. The next thing he knew he was free falling through a consuming gray. Dazed from lack of oxygen, he passed out. When he came to, he was falling head first. He didn't know how long he had been out. Was he falling through clouds or fog? If it was the latter, the ground was mere seconds away. He managed to pull the rip cord. His chute opened. As he floated earthward, he saw two other chutes. He called out to them. It turned out to be the co-pilot and engineer, both of whom had also escaped the aircraft. After the war, Robert would learn from an airman in a nearby bomber that the "We Dood It" exploded right after they bailed.

Suddenly, three German Messerschmitt 109s burst from the cloud ceiling and circled them. Every airman had heard stories of German pilots gunning down Allied chutists or chopping them up in their propellers. As the planes approached, Robert pulled his .45 auto pistol from its leather holster—a futile gesture against the razing guns of a ME-109. Despite the stories, there was a kind of chivalry between Allied and German pilots, a code of honor. We didn't shoot down their parachutes and they didn't shoot ours. Instead of firing on the three survivors, the Junker pilots circled for a while and radioed their location to ground spotters. After a few minutes, they tipped their wings at the chutists and saluted before returning to the aerial battle above the clouds.

Robert and the two other airmen were pretty certain that German soldiers would be waiting for them when they landed. Below them, they could see a small hamlet. Would the townspeople kill them on the spot or capture them as prisoners? He had heard stories of Allied airmen being hung from telegraph poles along roadways and left to rot in some of the cities that had suffered high death rates from bomb raids, cities like Berlin and Hamburg. Uncertain of the reception that awaited them, Robert kept his .45 handy. While slowly descending, Robert calculated that he must have fallen unconscious for about 20,000 feet. He thanked God that he woke up in time to pull the rip cord.

He dropped right into the center of the village, which turned out to be Obermkirchen. In fact, he landed right in the burgomaster's back yard. He and the other two airmen were immediately surrounded by armed soldiers and townspeople. Outnumbered and outgunned, Robert handed over his pistol. The Germans looked at Robert in disbelief. Here was an American enemy covered in blood who looked to be no older than sixteen. Some of the old women shook their heads and wept as they lamented in German, "So young. Boys. Just boys." They thought the blood covering him was his own. They were crying for him, for the suffering they thought he must be enduring.

Were these the vicious enemies Robert had heard about?

Robert spent his first two weeks as a prisoner of war in Dulag Luft in central Frankfurt, the starting point for many Allied prisoners. As Robert looked at the leveled city beyond the tiny window of his bare cell, he appreciated the irony that he had taken part in turning the city to rubble. Between January 25th and the 30th, he had seen Frankfurt from 30,000 feet in three separate bomb raids that demolished the heart of the city. For two weeks, he endured the isolation, despair, and interrogations. The interrogation room had a large swastika flag draped on the wall and a uniformed officer greeted him in perfect English. As a nineteen-year-old buck sergeant, Robert didn't really have anything secret or even useful to tell them, no matter how much they tried to wrench more information out of him. He was a small fish.

The German officer who interrogated Robert told him that he had lived in New Jersey before the war for five years, working as a commercial sky-writer. But in reality he had been a spy. Cameras secretly mounted on his airplane took thousands of photos of cities and military bases along the East Coast. The German officer asked him which base he was from in England, but Robert refused to answer. When the officer showed him an aerial photo of Grafton-Underwood with its distinctive "GU" at the end of the runway, Robert raised an eyebrow and the German knew his answer. It wasn't his first interrogation. In the end, the Germans decided that Robert was too far out of the loop to know anything useful. Much to Robert's relief they never resorted to torture.

After two weeks at Dulag Luft, Robert and thousands of other allied prisoners were herded into train cars and transported across Germany into German-occupied Russia. They were let off the train only once during the ten-day journey, one night in Berlin during an RAF bombing raid.

When they arrived at Stalag Luft VI on the Lithuanian border, the commandant told them that their war was over. But as far as Robert was concerned, the war was far from over. He would find a means to escape. Because of his slight build, Robert was one of the escape tunnel diggers, burrowing underground with a spoon and his fingers like a mole. Because of the high water table, Robert spent a good deal of time with half his body underwater. Unfortunately, none of the tunnels led to freedom. Without proper support braces, they collapsed. Eventually, there were dozens of aborted collapsed tunnels. And every time they were discovered, the camp commandant ordered punishments such as the withholding of Red Cross packages. In retrospect, it seemed that the camp officers knew that the prisoners were digging all these tunnels, but since no one had escaped, they looked the other way. After all, it kept the prisoners busy and out of trouble. For Robert and the other prisoners, it gave them hope.

In July of 1944, the Germans began evacuating Stalag Luft VI because, during the summer offensive, the Russians were regaining lost ground. The Germans feared the POW camp would be overrun. Therefore, the allied prisoners were again packed into train boxcars (standing up) and transported to the port of Memel on the Baltic Sea. There they were herded into the hold of a rusty Russian coal ship called the *Masuren*, complete with the Russian hammer and sickle emblazoned on the side. Robert and thousands of other allied prisoners were jammed like sardines when the large hatch was closed, pitching them in utter darkness. It was one of Robert's worse experiences as a prisoner of war. The men relieved themselves in buckets that were lowered and later hoisted out of the hold, spilling their sloshing contents on the men below in the process. Many of the men were sick and suffering from vomiting and diarrhea. It was horrible. Stripped of their humanity, prisoners in the dark hold felt like animals.

The Monk Who Fell From the Sky

Because the ship bore the Russian emblem, there was the real fear that German bombers might target it. They also worried that the ship might hit a mine. The *Masuren* took three days before it docked at Swinemunde. From there, the men were again herded into boxcars and transported to Kiefeheide, a small town near Poland. Unknown to the thousands of prisoners crammed into the boxcars, Hitler had ordered changes to the POW system. After "The Great Escape" at Stalag Luft III, where 50 prisoners were executed as deterrent to future attempts, the SS and Gestapo were to take control of all camps.

Before their forced march to Luft IV, their new POW camp, Robert and about a thousand other prisoners from the American Air Corps, as well as about eight hundred British and Canadian prisoners, were shackled in twos, ankle-to-ankle and wrist-to-wrist. Worse, soldiers with vicious dogs, SS, and even Kreigsmarines (the corps of German sailors) with fixed bayonets were to escort them to the camp. Hitler had given orders that any prisoner who tried to escape was to be shot. There would be no more escapes.

What happened next was like a terrible scene from a war movie.

The Gestapo ordered the prisoners, still bound awkwardly in shackles, to jog to the new camp, which was about two miles away. As they ran, the dogs menaced them, biting and tearing their legs and ankles; townspeople lining the narrow streets of Kiefeheide spat at them and hurled insults at them in German and occasionally in English. The men with bayonets jabbed at stragglers or battered them with the butts of their rifles. Some of the men who were suffering malnutrition and dehydration from vomiting and diarrhea fell back, too weak to keep up the pace. The dogs attacked those unfortunates, while others were beaten, kicked, or bayonetted as they lay on the ground exhausted and unable to take another step. As the Germans plunged their bayonets into the fallen prisoners, they shouted out the names of German cities that had been bombed into ruins.

"Eine fur Berlin!"

"Eine fur Hamburg!"

"Eine fur Koln!"

All the time, German soldiers shouted that they should try to escape, while soldiers with machine guns waited to cut down any man who broke from the column. Robert and the two thousand other prisoners felt they were going to be massacred.

The POWs did their best to aid one another, carrying, and even dragging those who couldn't keep up. Stronger runners moved to the outside edges of the column to protect the weaker ones in the center. By the time they finally reached Stalag Luft IV, some of the prisoners had as many as 50 bayonet wounds. Robert was struck by rifle butts a few times and managed to receive only two gashes from a bayonet. He never knew exactly how many prisoners were severely wounded or killed during the infamous "Heydekrug Run," one of the countless atrocities committed by the Nazis during the war.

Hundreds he suspected.

Life at Stalag Luft IV was very different from Luft VI. The Gestapo ran things with an iron thumb pressed down on the prisoner's fleeting hopes. For one thing, anyone caught trying to escape was summarily executed. For another, the barracks were all built above ground, so that it was impossible to dig tunnels without being seen. Food was scarcer than before. Hunger was a constant companion, never far from Robert's mind. As many as ten men would share a single loaf of bread that seemed to use sawdust as a main ingredient. The thin soup was made of dehydrated potatoes from the 1930s and had maggots in it. New prisoners plucked the maggots from their tin cup, but the prisoners who had been there longer closed their eyes and ate the soup, maggots and all. If a horse died, there might be a little meat in the soup. The coffee was terrible. The men joked it was made of burnt acorns. Robert took up smoking cigarettes to take away the lingering taste of the coffee. Everyone lost a lot of weight. Occasionally, a sympathetic German guard would give an extra ration of bread, even though the guards weren't eating much better than the prisoners.

The worst part of the boring, endless days was the uncertainty about what would happen next. At any moment, on any day, orders could come down to get rid of all the prisoners. The men knew that, and knew there was nothing they would be able to do to stop it.

After seven months at Luft IV, orders came down in February of 1945 to evacuate the camp as the Russians were closing in. Robert and the rest of the prisoners marched all the way to Hamburg, and by spring were housed in a deserted pottery factory in Annaberg, on the Elbe River. During an Allied air raid, all of the German guards ran away, seeking better cover. Robert and one of his pals, a guy named Vic, escaped into the countryside. Vic could speak a little Russian. They decided to head east, toward the Russians and away from the advancing Allied troops, out of fear they might be shot by accident. But they never forgot their duty to get a little revenge on the Germans, to cause a little chaos or destruction. Cutting German communication lines became a pastime.

Decades after the war, one of Robert's favorite movies was *The Great Escape* (1963) starring Steve McQueen, Charles Bronson, James Garner, Donald Pleasance, Richard Attenborough, and James Coburn, about American POW's escaping from a German Stalag. As much as any Hollywood production could, Robert said, the film accurately depicted life in a Stalag. Near the beginning of the movie, a captured

American officer reminds the camp commandant: "It is the sworn duty of American soldiers to try to escape their captor, to confound the enemy by forcing them to expend great resources to imprison and recapture them, and to harass the enemy at all times."

Robert's experience put that oath to the test.

Eventually, tired and hungry, Robert and Vic came upon a farmhouse outside Annaberg. Robert, who had learned a little German during his year of imprisonment, told the farmer that if he hid the two, then Vic, who spoke some Russian, would put in a good word for him when the Russians arrived. The family took them in, fed them, and hid them in the barn when a retreating German infantry division passed through. The two months with the family taught Robert that all Germans weren't evil. They were just like most families back home. Slowly, Robert's bitterness and hate dissolved. When the Red Army arrived on April 23, 1945, which was Robert's birthday, Vic told the Russians that the farmer had not only sheltered the two of them, but that he had also aided escaped Russian POWs.

The farmer's house and barn was the only one that wasn't burned to the ground.

At first Robert and Vic helped the Russians round up German soldiers, something which he would later regret. In their desire for revenge for what the Germans had done to Russia, the Russians were vicious. If a soldier was found with an SS tattoo, they were summarily executed. Many of the captured German soldiers were shipped to Russia as slaves to rebuild what they had destroyed. Many died in captivity. Some who survived did not see Germany again for years.

Robert witnessed many more atrocities in the two months he spent with the Russians than he had during his year as a German prisoner. Many of the atrocities were committed against German civilians. They savagely raped girls and women, forcing their brothers, sons, or husbands to watch. Robert remembered a time when a Russian soldier fired his machine gun into a house full of women without provocation. For years thereafter, he heard their pitiful screams in his nightmares.

Finally, in June of 1945, with the war over, the Russians released Robert and twenty-nine other Allied prisoners as part of a negotiation. Tears filled his eyes as he and the other men crossed a bridge on the Elbe River to rejoin American troops waiting on the other side.

He was going home.

Robert was awarded the Purple Heart for the wounds he suffered as a prisoner of war.

Over the next several years, Robert had a difficult time adjusting to civilian life. He couldn't keep a steady job. There were no jobs for experienced tail gunners in the real world. He had a few bad relationships and break-ups, probably related to his experiences in the war. Like so many young men returned from battle, Robert couldn't shake the horrors he had witnessed: the Germans bayonetting prisoners who fell behind during the forced run to Stalag Luft IV; the Russian's merciless revenge on all Germans at the end of the war; and his own role in leveling and firebombing entire German cities. Nightly, he awoke drenched in sweat from night terrors. Nowadays, he would probably be diagnosed with Post Traumatic Stress Disorder.

Like so many young men returning from WWII, Robert read Thomas Merton's *The Seven Storey Mountain*. The book inspired him. He was disillusioned by the vapid consumerism of post-war America. He wanted to live as Merton lived. He wanted the simplicity of a monk's life with its focus on labor, prayer, and contemplation. Most of all, perhaps what he and others like him sought was penance for their role in the war. Maybe even forgiveness. Maybe just the solace of forgetfulness. In 1951, Robert was admitted to The Abbey of Our Lady of Gethsemani as a monk and took on the monastic name of Irenaeus. At first, Br. Irenaeus was assigned to the Print Shop, where the abbey printed its own materials. Over the next few years, he learned how to operate and repair the machines. It was policy of the Abbey that the monks learned different trade skills. As such, their work assignments rotated.

(Br. Irenaeus on hydraulic cutter in the Print Shop)

Br. Irenaeus' next work assignment was in the abbey's Tailoring Shop, where he manufactured and repaired the clothing the monks wore, including their religious garments, like their cassocks and scapulars.

The Monk Who Fell From the Sky

(Br. Irenaeus measuring patterns in the Tailoring Shop)

As Brother Irenaeus, Robert would spend the next seventeen years laboring, sweating, eating, and praying alongside Thomas Merton and the hundred or so other men living at the Kentucky monastery. No matter what trades they learned, every monk also worked the fields to grow their food and to support the abbey. Like Merton and the other monks, Robert would learn the thousand year old sign language of the Cistercians, used to communicate while preserving the silence so essential to their order. In fact, it was because of the word "silence" that Merton chose to become a Trappist.

Robert was a poet at heart. During his years at the abbey, he wrote many poems, which he shared with Father Louis (Merton), who, aside from being his spiritual advisor, also performed as a kind of writing mentor.

By 1967, however, Robert was growing restless at Gethsemani. In his early forties, he wondered if he shouldn't do something different with the rest of his life. He prayed to God to send him a sign.

(Br. Irenaeus tossing hay bales up to a fellow monk, c. 1960, from *Gethsemani: A Life of Praise*)

The Intrepid Little Nun

Around the time Robert joined the poor monks at the Trappist monastery of Gethsemani a few miles south of Bardstown, Kentucky, a young woman in New Jersey was beginning a path that would lead her to the same place. In both life trajectories, Thomas Merton played a significant role. It almost seemed as if the lives and legacies of all three were destined to be intertwined in a way that would endure for more than half a century after Merton's death.

But to tell her story truly, we must start at the beginning where one tragedy was compounded by another, suffering heaped on suffering.

Helen Marie was born near East Conemaugh, Pennsylvania in December of 1932. Conemaugh is renowned for the almost biblically cataclysmic 1889 "Johnstown Flood." In his book *The Johnstown Flood: The Incredible Story behind One of the Most Devastating Disasters America Has Ever Known* (1968), David McCullough, the two-time Pulitzer Prize winning social historian described the event succinctly:

> At the end of the last century, Johnstown, Pennsylvania was a booming coal-and-steel town filled with hardworking families striving for a piece of the nation's burgeoning industrial prosperity. In the mountains above John-

stown, an old earth dam had been hastily rebuilt to create a lake for an exclusive summer resort patronized by the tycoons of that same industrial prosperity, among them Andrew Carnegie, Henry Clay Frick, and Andrew Mellon. Despite [numerous] warnings of possible danger, nothing was done about the dam. Then came May 31, 1889, when [after days of relentless rainfall] the dam burst, sending a wall of water thundering down the mountain, smashing through [East Conemaugh and] Johnstown, and killing more than 2,000 people.

McCullough goes on to describe the errors that caused the disaster and retells the horrific consequences. The earth dam had been built to hold back nothing larger or deeper than a pond. Once the South Fork Fishing and Hunting Club was established as a summer playground for rich tycoons, the dam was put to the test as the lake level was increased year after year until a three mile long by one mile wide lake was held back. Over the years, the dam sprung leaks, which were shoddily repaired. For some of the townsfolk, it was only a matter of time before the dam would break. It finally did, bursting open on May 31, 1889, releasing a wall of water more than seventy feet high which raced down the valley of the South Fork Creek, turned west where it joined the Little Conemaugh River, and, at speeds of more than forty miles per hour, slammed into a viaduct. Because the valley narrowed, the rushing wall of water was seventy-six feet tall. Within minutes, the tiny hamlets of East Conemaugh, Franklin, and Woodmill were all but wiped off the face of the earth.

The Intrepid Little Nun

(Ruins of the Sisters of Charity Building)

When the wall finally hit Johnstown at the confluence of Stony Creek and the Little Conemaugh, the water cut through town like a bulldozer before it slammed up against the Pennsylvania Rail Road Bridge where all the flotsam carried in the deluge clogged the river's downriver course, creating a giant whirlpool, twenty-three feet deep. The desperate living and more than a thousand corpses swirled in the vortex. There was no escape for the living. If they did not soon drown, they were killed in the floating, grinding debris. The same is often said about tornadoes: It's not the high winds that kill you, but the debris in the wind. As if matters couldn't get worse, the flotsam of wooden buildings snagged against the stone bridge caught fire from oil spilled from an upended railroad tanker. Survivors from the initial flood were burned alive as they clamored to escape the raging inferno. From shore, bystanders heard their pitiful screams for help, but could do nothing.

(Debris piled against the P. R. R. Bridge)

In the aftermath, nearly a thousand bodies that had been recovered from the mud and debris were unidentifiable. All too often, only an arm or leg or headless torso was found. Today, a cemetery for those unknown dead sits on a hill above the town overlooking the river that killed them. News of the devastating flood shocked and galvanized America. Donations and volunteers poured in. It was one of the first tests of Clara Barton's newly established Red Cross.

Helen Marie was born in the back of a coal miner's shack in East Conemaugh forty-three years after the flood that had obliterated the town. Her mother was Slavic and often spoke Slavic at home. Many of the families in Conemaugh were Slavic immigrants. Her father was a poor Italian-American coal miner who never seemed to get ahead. No matter how hard he worked, his "American Dream" was always slipping away from him, as if swept away by the river that had once swept away the entire town and everyone that lived in it. He suffered debilitating migraines after a head injury caused when the mine shaft he was working in collapsed. Several of his co-workers were less fortunate. Afterward, her father started drinking to ease the pain.

In 1935 or 36, during a binge, her father doused the small house in kerosene and set it ablaze while five year old Helen Marie and her three year old brother and their mother were sleeping. To this day, Helen Marie believes her father did it to "put them out of *his* misery." He was arrested and thrown into jail. When he sobered up in his cell, he remembered what he had done. Thinking he had killed his entire family, he hung himself with his belt.

No one had told him that his wife and children had escaped the fire.

Little Helen Marie, clutching her mother's dress, accompanied her mother to the jail to identify her father's body. She never forgot seeing her father's corpse lying on the cot. When the sheriff asked her mother if she wanted to claim the body for burial, she responded, "Why? He left us with nothing. Not even enough money to bury him."

After that, her mother moved the family to New Jersey.

(Helen Marie [left] and siblings, c. 1937;
Photo used with permission)

In her late teens, Helen Marie looked a lot like Audrey Hepburn, the girl who went on to be one of the most glamorous actresses of the time, starring in such iconic movies as *Breakfast at Tiffany's, Roman Holiday, My Fair Lady, Gigi,* and *Sabrina.* Hepburn in 1959 turned down a role in *The Diary of Anne Frank* because, as a girl in the Netherlands, she had witnessed Nazis rounding up and executing Jews in the streets and worried that playing in the film might bring back painful childhood memories. Hepburn was later considered for the main role in *Cleopatra,* which eventually went to Elizabeth Taylor. (Hepburn and Taylor were among the first actresses to be paid a million dollars for their roles.) Young Helen Marie frequently dressed like Audrey Hepburn and even staged photographs that resembled photos of her.

(Audrey Hepburn [above] and Helen Marie [below], c. 1952; Photo credit of Ms. Hepburn: Google Commons)

(Helen Marie in New York City, c. 1952)

Around the same time that Robert joined Thomas Merton and the other monks at the Abbey of Gethsemani as Brother Irenaeus, Helen Marie was dating a man named Frank Semica, who came from a wealthy New Jersey family. One day, Frank asked Helen Marie to marry him. A dutiful Catholic girl, Helen Marie went to church to pray and to ask for guidance. While kneeling before the statue of Mary, Helen Marie had an ecstatic vision in which the statue of Mary suddenly came alive and told her not to marry, but instead to devote her life to serving God. Young Helen Marie had read about Teresa of Avila's ecstatic visions in Spain. She took the vision to mean that she should become a nun.

(Helen Marie and Frank Semica in New Jersey, c. 1952)

Frank took the news hard.

Her mother was elated.

Within the year, Helen Marie joined the Sisters Adorers of the Precious Blood, a cloistered convent at 5400 Fort Hamilton Parkway in Brooklyn, New York. The sisters referred to themselves as the handmaidens of Jesus. Active nuns are the ones you see wearing habits and going about in the public sphere doing Church related duties, including working at soup kitchens, church-run thrift stores, and the likes. Cloistered nuns, like the cloistered monks at Gethsemani, almost never leave the isolation of their walled monasteries. They spend their lives isolated (some might say *insulated* or *sheltered*) within the confines of their monastery grounds laboring and praying. Helen Marie often recounted in interviews that "as a contemplative, you are always praying for the whole world."

The Mother Superior told Helen Marie that she had been praying for a new, young nun as the convent had been shorthanded for some time. Helen Marie was the answer to her prayers.

As is the tradition when taking vows to join a Catholic order, Helen Marie took a religious name, just as Robert had done when he became Brother Irenaeus and as Thomas Merton had done when he became Father Louis. At the moment she took her vows, Helen Marie became Sister Mary Pius, named after Pope Pius X (1835-1914; Pontiff from 1903-1914). She said it was not a name she would have chosen for herself. On the day she took her vows, her brother took her out to celebrate with a banana split.

For the next thirteen or fourteen years, Sister Mary Pius spent her long and tiring days laboring and praying. A large board announced each nun's chores for the day. Sister Mary Pius always seemed to have more chores than the other nuns. To this day, she believes that

Mother Catherine did it to keep her busy and out of trouble.

"Idle hands are the devil's workshop," she was always saying.

For the most part, Sister Mary Pius' duties were in the kitchen. She was a scullery maid, cooking, cleaning, setting tables, and washing dishes. When asked if she had cooked much before, Mary Pius had answered that she had not, to which Mother Catherine replied, "No matter. The Lord will provide."

But Mary Pius was also sometimes assigned to work in the gardens or to scrub floors.

The nuns would all go to bed around 9 p.m., only to awaken at midnight to gather in the chapel to recite the Divine Office and to sing or chant the Psalms. After an hour, they would return to their cells to sleep again before getting up at 5 a.m. to start another long day in the life of a contemplative. The monks at Gethsemani had a similar austere routine. The life of a cloistered contemplative, be it monastery or convent, is no picnic.

(Sister Mary Pius, right, and a fellow Sister at the monastery of the Sisters Adorers of the Precious Blood, c. 1953)

The Intrepid Little Nun

Sometimes Sister Mary Pius' brother or mother would give her a little spending cash, which she hid so that she could sometimes sneak out of the monastery at night and go see a late movie, especially ones starring her doppelganger, Audrey Hepburn. She loved movies. More than once, Mother Catherine found her bed empty when it should have contained a pious sleeping nun. Half a century later, Helen Marie was convinced that's one of the reasons why the Mother Superior always assigned her more work than the other nuns.

She remembers looking at the assignment board with all her chores, and asking about the discrepancy: "Excuse me, Mother Catherine. I think there's been some mistake with the board," she'd say humbly. "I seem to have too many duties for the day."

"Oh, there's no mistake," the Mother Superior would reply without looking at the board.

During the years that Helen Marie, a.k.a. Sister Mary Pius, lived at the Brooklyn convent, her mother enjoyed taking little "vacations" where she stayed in one of the guest rooms at the convent and was pampered by the nuns.

It seemed that the liberal spirit of America in the 1960s spilled over the brick walls and into the convent. Many of the young nuns were secretly reading Merton, swapping books, and whispering about him. Their admiration was secret because Merton was seen as too progressive by the older nuns and the Mother Superior.

In late 1966, after fourteen years as a nun at the convent in Brooklyn, Helen Marie felt a burning desire to meet Merton and to learn from him. She had been having doubts about her life in the convent. She didn't know what to do with the rest of her life. She desperately wanted a spiritual teacher to help guide her. Other nuns told her that someone as famous as Thomas Merton wouldn't make time for someone like her—an uneducated scullery maid who had spent her vocation washing and scouring dishes in the convent kitchen.

Apparently, they didn't know Sister Mary Pius very well.

She was an intrepid and feisty force to reckon with.

The little nun made a New Year's resolution to meet Thomas Merton.

In the early days of January 1967, Helen Marie went to speak with Father Campbell, the stereotypical Irish Catholic priest who served as Abbot at the convent and pastor at the adjacent Catholic church. Over the years, he had become Sister Mary Pius's friend and confessor. She related her desire to meet Merton, certain that the "Good Father" would try to dissuade her as had her fellow sisters. To her amazement and relief, Father Campbell encouraged her to go, albeit with a proviso, namely, that she not write or call the Abbey of Gethsemani to arrange a visit. Instead, he urged her just to go. Just show up on their doorsteps. It would be more difficult for them to turn away a nun who had traveled half way across America. In a gesture of his support, the Abbot reached into his own wallet and gave her the money for round-trip Greyhound bus tickets and meals. Helen Marie never told me what she said or did not say about her plan to Mother Superior, who most certainly would have forbidden her to leave the convent on such a foolhardy adventure–unless overruled by the Abbot. To this day, I can't help but imagine that the crafty little nun placed pillows under her bedsheets to resemble her sleeping form to fool the abbess long enough to make her escape. I do not know if she disclosed her secret plan to any of her fellow nuns.

I am inclined to think that she did not.

The Intrepid Little Nun

On Friday evening, January 12, 1967, after a long and eventful journey that began at Manhattan's Port Authority Building and included a few mix-ups along the way, Sister Mary Pius showed up at Gethsemani's gate during the biggest snow storm in years. She was met by an elderly woman named Mrs. Gannon who escorted her to a room in the abbey's guest house. After asking to see Thomas Merton, the little nun was bombarded with questions to which the abbot demanded answers, such as where did she come from? Which nunnery did she belong to? Why hadn't she written in advance before traveling so far? And finally, what business did she have with Father Louis (Merton)? Worried that they might send her away after she had come so far, the little nun spilled the beans. She told them everything, including how Father Campbell back in Brooklyn had directed her to travel to the abbey without notice and how he had even given her bus money from his own pocket.

The hour was already late. Sister Mary Pius had no means by which to go back to Bardstown or Louisville at such an hour. So the abbot did the only decent thing he could do under the circumstances—he put her up for the night in their guest house outside the walled monastery.

For two days, Sister Mary Pius waited in the guest house for Merton to come see her. But she was told he was at his hermitage up in the hills, and that, because of the snow, he wasn't going to see her. But the little nun was determined. She wasn't going home without meeting Thomas Merton.

And so she waited.

On Saturday afternoon, Mr. and Mrs. Gannon came to inform Helen Marie that Fr. Louis would meet with her Sunday morning from 11 a.m. to 11:30 a.m. Helen Marie was so excited that she barely slept that night from thinking of all the things she wanted to say to Merton.

Merton showed up as scheduled. He had heard how far she had come to meet him. He told her that he admired her tenacity. Despite the planned thirty minutes, they sat and talked in the guest house parlor for a couple of hours, and it was decided that she would return to the nunnery in Brooklyn and that he, Thomas Merton, would work with the powers that be back home to get her reassigned closer to Gethsemani so that he could become her spiritual teacher and adviser. On Saturday night, after the Gannons had delivered the good news that Merton would see her, and while the transpiring events of her visit were still fresh in her mind, Helen Marie sat down at the small desk in the guest room and excitedly wrote a four-page letter to her mother and sister on Abbey of Gethsemani stationery. For reasons I do not fully understand, she never mailed it. Maybe she wrote it like a diary simply to preserve the faithfulness of the memory while the events were fresh in her mind—a contemporaneous record of sorts, a keepsake of her grand adventure. The handwritten letter begins:

(Sat.) Jan. 13, 1967

Beloved in Jesus & Mary: Hi Mom and Ann,

Grace, peace and joy be yours abundantly in Love Incarnate! May God be praised! At long last I made it. Arrived at 5:15 p.m. Friday evening. There was a bit of a mix up on the way due to the fact that Gethsemani is not located at the place I was told it was, which meant I had to buy 2 additional Greyhound tickets to get me there. This misinformation caused me a 5 hr. wait (from 2 a.m. – 7 a.m.) at Cincinnati to Louisville, and then another 4 hr. wait

The Intrepid Little Nun 67

at Louisville to get another bus at Bardstown. Actually, if I had remained on the bus at Cin. to Louisville I would have made it at least 8 hrs. sooner, if not more.

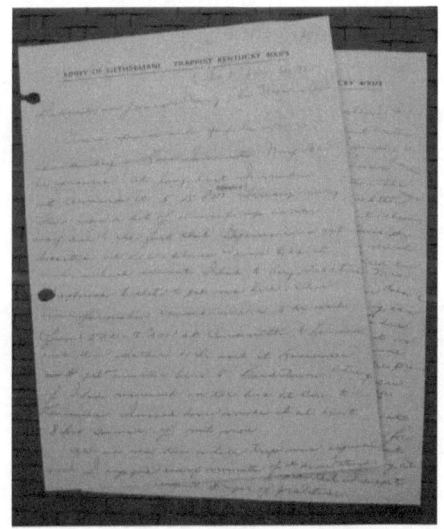

(Helen Marie's letter from the Guest House)

On page four of the letter, Helen Marie wrote how she felt about the thirty minutes that had been originally allotted to her visit with Merton after traveling so far: "A half hr. is too little, but I leave that all up to Jesus & Mary. They must speak in me & through me if it's going to [a]mount to anything. It's for them that I'm here."

After her meeting with Merton, Sister Mary Pius returned to Brooklyn. She excitedly related her adventures to Father Campbell and her sister nuns. True to his word, Father Louis wrote to Sister Mary Pius' superiors requesting dispensation (special consideration/allowance) for her to be transferred closer to the Abbey of Gethsemani. While awaiting dispensation, the excited nun wrote to Merton several times, thanking him for his help and reiterating her eagerness to begin what she called "a fresh new start."

In no time at all, Sister Mary Pius found herself assigned to the Sisters of Loretto Motherhouse in Nerinx, a mere thirteen miles from Gethsemani. At the Motherhouse, young Lorettines prepared to take their vows, and after spending their lives teaching or nursing, aged ones came back to rest, die and be buried in a beautiful cemetery up on the hill. Sister Mary Pius was granted dispensation from her convent back in Brooklyn, a formal sabbatical, of sorts. She was further instructed that she could not wear her religious habit during this period, though she was required to uphold her vows and religious observations.

(St. Joseph's Infirmary, Loretto Motherhouse, 1967.
Nowadays, the trees are so tall they obscure the building)

Helen Marie's mother was disappointed that she moved to Kentucky to be closer to Thomas Merton, because it brought an end to her little pampered vacations.

For the next two years Helen Marie worked in St. Joseph's Infirmary at the motherhouse caring for elderly nuns. During that time, she wrote often to Father Campbell back in Brooklyn. Every Sunday she and other nuns took a bus for the thirteen-mile ride to Gethsemani to attend Mass. At Gethsemani, Helen Marie met a monk by the name of Brother Irenaeus, who had been living at the monastery for fifteen years. He ran the Tailoring Shop at the monastery. As a kind of quartermaster of clothing, his duties required making religious habits and issuing and repairing clothes for fellow monks as needed. His "shop" was surrounded by shelves laden with shoes and socks, denim shirts and blue jeans, and habits of all sizes. He also stored the monks' "worldly" clothes (their civvies) and their trunks bearing the belongings with which they arrived at the gate of Gethsemani. With respect specifically to Merton, Br. Irenaeus was also responsible for storing the famous monk's suits, needed for those occasions when he left Gethsemani to go into the world. In addition he also repaired clothing damaged during the course of manual labor around the monastery, which was herculean. Physical labor, contemplation, the rigorous observance of ritual, chant, and silence comprise the hallmarks of Trappist monks.

(Brother Irenaeus at the Abbey of Gethsemani, c. 1967)

Like many young men who had been in WWII, Br. Irenaeus sought a place of quiet refuge where he could escape the recurring horrors and scars of combat and search for meaning and, perhaps even, forgiveness (Merton writes about this in *The Seven Storey Mountain*). Robert, as we have explained, had been a tail gunner in the Army Air Corps. After all his experiences in the war, he probably suffered from "Battle Fatigue," or what we would now call PTSD.

After Mass, Thomas Merton (Fr. Louis), Helen Marie (Sister Mary Pius), and Robert (Br. Irenaeus) would go for Sunday drives around the countryside in the monastery's doorless, four-wheel-drive Ford Bronco, looking for a good place to picnic. Brother Irenaeus was ordered to go along as a chaperone, as required by the abbots of both the monastery and the nunnery. Brother Irenaeus always did the driving because Thomas Merton didn't know how to drive. Many years before, he had tried to learn to drive one of the monastery's jeeps, but managed to crash it several times into trees and even overturned it. He never drove again. On their outings, Brother Irenaeus always drove while Helen Marie sat on the passenger side, with Merton sandwiched in the middle, the three jouncing into one another whenever the jeep hit bumps or potholes or ruts in the road. At such times, Helen Marie hung on for dear life, certain that she'd fall out. She still laughs when she thinks about those Sunday drives at Gethsemani.

Over all those Sundays, a friendship was forged among the three.

The Intrepid Little Nun 71

(Brother Irenaeus waiting for Sister Mary Pius by the frozen pond at Sisters of Loretto Motherhouse, 1967)

Sometimes after Mass, Helen Marie joined others at Merton's hermitage to listen to the famous monk talk about religion, spirituality, civil rights, and about his thoughts on the war. Although Helen Marie hitched a ride to Mass with other nuns, she alone stayed at Gethsemani for much of the rest of the afternoon, and, therefore, frequently had to walk the thirteen miles home to Loretto. (Even in her mid-80s, she still took long walks daily.) Did I mention that this little woman was determined? Sometimes Merton visited the Loretto Motherhouse to talk to the nuns about religion, spirituality, meditation, and the inner life of a contemplative. The nuns would play the piano and they'd all sing hymns or psalms. Merton seemed to enjoy the visits.

(Brother Irenaeus and Sister Mary Pius during a Sunday visit at the Abbey of Gethsemani, 1967-1968. Photo by Thomas Merton)

Merton was sometimes invited to speak in Louisville. On such occasions, he would wear his civilian suit and tie and patent leather dress shoes, what he called his "togs." In fact, included in the trunks was a handwritten note from Merton to Brother Irenaeus that instructed: "I'm going into the city. Please lay out my usual togs."

Merton would arrange for transportation from the abbey for the drive into Louisville. At least twice that Helen Marie could recall, always on a Friday or Saturday, Merton stopped at the Sisters of Loretto Motherhouse to take her along. She had been directed to dress incognito as well. After his talk, Merton and Helen Marie would go to a jazz club downtown. Merton always liked jazz. During his years in New York City before becoming a monk, he frequented happening establishments like Birdland. Helen Marie also liked jazz. They walked in dressed in their civvies and were seated by a host. Shortly thereafter, a waitress asked Merton what he wanted to drink. Helen Marie couldn't remember for certain, but she thought he ordered a gin and tonic or a scotch on the rocks. Turning to Helen Marie the attendant asked, "And what'll it be for the misses?"

The Intrepid Little Nun

Helen Marie always ordered a Shirley Temple with a maraschino cherry.

As the waitress walked away, they both laughed at the absurdity of them being mistaken for husband and wife. If only the waitress knew they were a monk and a nun incognito.

One has to wonder what the Abbot of Gethsemani and the Mother Superior at the convent would have thought of the couple's evening excursions and their disregard for their instructions to be discreet. But then, Thomas Merton and Sister Mary Pius were always rule-breakers in their own way. Merton was that rare American Trappist allowed to have his own hermitage away from his brother monks in the abbey; and Sister Mary Pius was known to climb out her window at the convent in Brooklyn to go watch late night movies.

Almost half a century later, during our visit to Louisville in January of 2016, Helen Marie recognized the district where she and Merton went to the Jazz Club, but the precise building eluded her memory. To be fair, there are few if any Jazz clubs nowadays. Most of the restaurants in the downtown district are trendy bars, bistros, or pizzerias designed to attract locals and tourists coming and going from the many activities at the conference center, or sporting events at the arena. I know. We ate at a few of them. Helen Marie thought one place in particular might have been the Jazz club "back in the day," but she wasn't sure. The place is not far from where nowadays there stands the famous sign at the intersection of Fourth and Walnut describing the moment Thomas Merton was suddenly filled with an unshakable and selfless love for everyone around him.

(Sister Mary Pius and Brother Irenaeus at Gethsemani, 1967-1968; Photo by Thomas Merton)

From January 1967 up until he left on his Asian Journey in the fall of 1968, Thomas Merton became Helen Marie's personal spiritual teacher and confidant. More than that, they were friends. Their friendship became close enough that Helen Marie confided in him and confessed to him, and he, in turn, came to trust her enough to confide in her. He told her things he may have never told his male friends or brother monks.

It is a fact that as a young man, Merton had a weakness for women. As an undergraduate student at Cambridge University, he was known to be quite the drinker and philanderer. In 1934, he left Cambridge in a hurry, ostensibly because of girl trouble, and moved to New York City where he enrolled at Columbia University and eventually earned a bachelor's and a master's degree. In April 1966, at the age of 51, Merton developed a close and controversial relationship with Margie Smith, a student nurse he met at a hospital in Louisville after he underwent surgery for debilitating back pain. At 26, Margie was half his age.

The Intrepid Little Nun 75

This is not to imply in any way that the relationship between Thomas Merton and Helen Marie was inappropriate in nature. I am convinced such was not the case. It is evident to me that their relationship was that of a teacher and student. But more than that, they were friends. Merton might have felt safe talking to Helen Marie in a way he didn't feel comfortable with other men. I understand his feeling, for I have always been so inclined in my own life. My father often criticized me for it when I was a young man.

"Why don't you hang around with guys more?" he used to grumble.

A half-blood Alaska Native and a decorated Army soldier who served two tours in Vietnam (one at the beginning and one at the end; he retired as a Lt. Colonel), and a man renowned as a tough-as-nails outdoorsman who could endure more hardship than most men could ever withstand, my father embodied *machismo*. He even looked a little like Clint Eastwood, one of his favorite actors when I was growing up. My father would have been a good Spartan.

Deeply religious as it was, Gethsemani was still a community of men. Men are men, no matter the circumstance. Regardless of intent, humility, and piety, the men at Gethsemani were still creatures of their American upbringing, given to the same masculine insecurities and bravado as all men.

Merton occasionally confided to Helen Marie about his feelings about Margie Smith, despite the fact that the "affair" had ended by the time Helen Marie arrived at Gethsemani in January of 1967. But despite the saying that "Time heals all wounds," six months is not enough time to heal a broken heart. I know that from experience. A competing axiom says that "Absence makes the heart grow fonder." Perhaps the memory of the fresh "scandal" is what led Mrs. Gannon, the old lady who managed the monastery's guest house, to ask Helen Marie what business she had with Thomas Merton.

It is sad to say that Helen Marie may have been the *only* person Father Louis could confide in about his feelings for Margie Smith. He certainly could not speak to his fellow brethren for fear of rebuke, scorn, rejection, or alienation . . . and possibly out of fear of being defrocked. I know that if gossip travels like wild fire in the outside world, it races through cloistered communities like a raging wild fire fanned by a whirlwind. Despite the commandment not to bear false witness against your neighbor (gossip can be included as a kind of "false witness"), from the beginning of her mentor-student relationship with Merton, other nuns at the Loretto Motherhouse warned Helen Marie about Merton. They cautioned her to watch out for him, reciting the tired gossip about his relationship with Margie Smith the previous spring and summer. Brother Irenaeus and other monks at Gethsemani similarly warned her, recounting how some of Merton's phone conversations with the young nurse had been overhead by other monks who inadvertently, or not, had picked up another telephone receiver on the same line and quietly listened in on what was said. Or they listened from around a corner. Either way, it is clear to me that Merton was judged by his fellow and neighboring contemplatives.

If I have learned anything from my close friendships with clergy from many faiths and denominations, it is that, despite their elevated status in society, they are still human beings, prone to our collective shortcomings such as the propensity to judge others and to spread rumors, especially those of a salacious nature.

It is also clear to me that, despite the many decades since his death, Thomas Merton is still being judged.

The Intrepid Little Nun

When I traveled to the Thomas Merton Center in Louisville to share news of my "discovery" of his personal effects, a visiting scholar in the Merton Library overheard me talking excitedly to the director about the artifacts in the collection.

"I have that object in the collection," I said, pointing to some picture on the wall or on a book cover.

"I also have that object," I said pointing elsewhere.

I could tell the man was eavesdropping, which, because the room wasn't that big, wasn't hard to do. At one point, he approached me and, looking me over, he asked me if my mother was Margie Smith. I think he thought I might have been the love child of Thomas Merton and Margie Smith and that I must have inherited the collection of objects from my mother. To be fair to him, I was about the right age, and Helen Marie often told me that I reminded her of Merton. At the time, I hadn't heard about the relationship, and I must have had an oblivious look on my face.

Paul Pearson immediately corrected the man.

"No, he's not Margie's son," he said sharply, fearful of a rumor starting in the world of Thomas Merton studies.

If I have learned anything about human nature, it is that it does not change just because a person decides to take religious vows or to sequester oneself within a pious, cloistered community. After a quarter century hidden away from the world, I believe Merton wrestled with his legitimate feelings for Margie Smith. What would have been worse would have been if he had *not* wrestled with his human nature and his desire to be touched and held and loved.

Though times may change, Man will forever be Man. Thousands of generations have not altered our essential nature in the slightest.

Even talking about the subject of Merton and the nurse half a century later made Helen Marie uncomfortable and withdrawn. It was the only time in all the years I interviewed her that I could tell I was probing an area of her friendship with Merton that she had hoped to avoid talking about altogether. She didn't want to offer much more than to indicate that other nuns and monks had cautioned her about the relationship, and to acknowledge that she and Father Louis had occasionally spoken about it. She gave me no reason to believe that Fr. Louis had been unfaithful to his vows, only that he had profound emotions that he hadn't felt in decades and needed someone to talk to. On separate occasions, Helen Marie told me that Fr. Louis would make her promise never to repeat anything he said to her in confidence.

"Don't ever quote me anywhere," he said, "or I'll deny it."

Helen Marie remained true to her promise never to disclose what the two of them talked about during their visits.

We should all have friends like that.

When it came to any confession by Thomas Merton about his feelings for Margie Smith—unrequited love, a temporary judgment of error, or otherwise—Helen Marie could understand him. As a nun, she was developing similar feelings for Brother Irenaeus, feelings which she confessed to Merton and sought his advice about. For his part, Brother Irenaeus also sought Merton's guidance about his growing feelings for Sister Mary Pius.

All three were suffering from lovesickness in one form or another.

A nun through and through, Helen Marie especially wrestled with how her earthly love for another human being might impact her love for God and Jesus. In taking their vows, nuns—so tradition says—are married to Jesus. Many times she and Robert had long discussions about the issue. In a letter written on Abbey of Gethsemani stationery on September 8, 1968—one month before Merton left for his Asian Journey—Brother Irenaeus promised Helen Marie that he would never allow her love for him to come between her love for God and Jesus. In a postscript at the top of the letter, he informed Sister Mary Pius that he was to have a meeting that Tuesday at 1:40 p.m. with Abbot Flavian to discuss his desire to get married. In the letter, he declared his love for her:

> "My love for you, my darling, grows more intense every day. With each passing hour it grows deeper, more pure and holy, for it comes right from the heart of Christ. Please never ever fear that my love for you, or yours for me, will ever come between me and God, or be a hindrance in any way. Quite the contrary. Your pure and virginal love for me is teaching me more about God's love than I could have learned in a lifetime.... In loving each other, we love God more, just as in loving God more and attaining a more intimate union with Him, we are enabled to love each other more and to attain a more intimate union with each other, both now and for all eternity.... I send you my deepest, purest love my darling, my Mary. The letter ends, "Your Joseph, Br. m. Irenaeus."

> P.S. – I am scheduled to see
> Fr. Flavian on Tues at 1:40
> so please you are in prayer
> that he will be inspired as he
> was on Pentecost.
>
> **ABBEY OF GETHSEMANI**
> TRAPPIST, KENTUCKY
>
> Sept 8th
>
> Mary's Birthday, 1968
>
> My Beloved One,
>
> I'm going to retire early tonight so I won't have time to start Butterworth's tape or to begin reading the things you gave me, though I am anxious to read them.
> Instead, I thought I would drop you a little note to thank you with all my heart for today....for all the wonderful things you said and did, and for the tremendous inspiration, hope and joy you instilled in my heart. I just know that all you are working for, and that I am working and praying for, is going to take root within me and help me to soar to those lofty heights of love and union which you have already attained. I want to be there, not because of you, but because of Him, the God of Love Who is calling me. But I want to be there with you, my precious angel, my other self, to experience it and share it with you. A joy shared is a joy enriched, and this is even more true in spiritual matters. You are my Polaris, my North Star, guiding me across the darkened wastelands of my unknowing. And, whereas before...

(Br. Irenaeus' letter to Sister Mary Pius)

Brother Irenaeus could not have known at the time he was writing that letter just how long Helen Marie would hold him to his remarkable and unconventional promise to protect her "virginal love" for him.

In the weeks and months before he left on his Asian journey, Merton counselled them both that they should get married if that's what they really wanted. Brother Irenaeus' meeting with the abbot was one more step in that direction.

Merton told them, "Priests and nuns don't have a monopoly on serving God. You can still devote your life to serving God as laypeople."

On some level, he might have been counselling himself.

After all, all three friends were human beings. Though their hearts were unquestionably filled with love and devotion to God, each still yearned for a more tangible love such as the reassuring touch of a hand or the comforting sanctuary of a warm embrace. It didn't matter that they were a priest, a monk, or a nun. After decades of life in their respective cloistered communities—sixty years combined—they each yearned for a soulmate, fully aware of what that might mean to their future as religious.

Merton reminded Helen Marie often that what he said to her in confidence must never be repeated. As far as I can tell, she kept her end of the bargain. She disclosed certain things to me only after half a century passed since her mentor's death, and because in her mid-80s, she worried that her own end couldn't be far off. She wanted the story that history will tell about the life and death of Thomas Merton to be accurate. For years, she prayed to Merton to send someone to her who could help her, not only with the disposition of his belongings, but someone who could tell her story to the world. Most importantly, she beseeched Merton to send her someone who could tell his story to the world. Helen Marie absolutely believes that her beloved teacher wants this story told.

Providence seemed to have lent a helping hand, if not a helpful shove.

Over the two years he knew her, Merton came to admire the simple, genuine, unfettered, yet passionate spiritualism of Helen Marie and the other nuns at the Loretta Motherhouse who came to Gethsemani for Mass and for other annual Catholic observances. In fact, Merton wrote about them in his *Asian Journal* on the evening before he left Dharmsala after his visits with the Dalai Lama:

> "The sky is reddening behind the big spur of mountains to the east. The days here have been good ones. Plenty of time for reading and meditation, and some extraordinary encounters. So far my talks with Buddhists have been open and frank and there has been full communication on a really deep level. We seem to recognize in one

another a certain depth of spiritual experience, and it is unquestionable. On this level I find in the Buddhists a deeper attainment of certitude than in Catholic contemplatives. On the other hand, in Catholics, such as the nuns of Loretto Motherhouse . . . the desire is deep and genuine and so too is a certain attainment, even though it is much less articulate." (124)

Helen Marie was precisely the kind of person with whom Thomas Merton needed to associate—a modern-thinking Catholic who embraced a spirituality of love, compassion, and mercy for everyone, not just for fellow Catholics or Christians, not of exclusivity, but of wholeness, common ground, and all-embracing love for all people, indeed for all living things. She might have been a bit of a hippy nun. But then, there was a little bit of hippy in Thomas Merton. Like her mentor, Helen Marie understood that the contemplative life compels us to action to help alleviate pain and suffering in others through acts of compassion and social justice. Like Merton, Helen Marie understood that love is the great action that saves and redeems us. But he also needed her as a confidant to confess the kinds of things he could not easily share with his brother monks, like his complex feelings about Margie Smith.

Merton trusted the Sister so much that in the days before he embarked for Southeast Asia, he asked her to meet him by the statue of Joseph outside the walls of the abbey. He wanted to confess something to her, and he didn't want anyone else to overhear what he had to say. As usual, Brother Irenaeus acted as a chaperone, but Merton requested that the monk stand far enough away so that he could not hear what was said.

On that little hill, with the smell of freshly cut hay on the wind, Thomas Merton divulged his secret, a secret she would safeguard for the next half century . . . a secret that had the potential to change history. Before leaving, Merton gave his friend a personal gift to remember him by. The two hugged before rejoining their ever-present chaperone. Brother Irenaeus saw that the little nun had tears in her eyes.

It was the last time Helen Marie saw Thomas Merton alive.

The Abbot's Orders

Word of Thomas Merton's death arrived at the Abbey of Gethsemani via telegram on the very day of his mysterious death in Bangkok. The tragic news spread quickly throughout the monastery. Merton's body was returned to America on December 17, 1968 via a military transport plane along with the bodies of dead American soldiers returning home from Vietnam. The sad irony is that Merton had worked so hard to end the war, and yet his death ended up being bound forever to the corpses of young men returning home as casualties of war. A funeral service was immediately held. A dated Pan American Airlines cargo receipt shows that Merton's personal effects, that is, the luggage he took with him on his journey, didn't arrive until January 16, 1969, almost a month after his death.

By then, Merton's funeral service had concluded. Both Brother Irenaeus and Sister Mary Pius attended the small funeral service. They also attended the Mass for Thomas Merton where Abbot Flavian read his eulogy. Both were present for the burial service as well. In fact, Brother Irenaeus drove over to the Sisters of Loretto Motherhouse to pick up Sister Mary Pius and a few other nuns for the service.

It struck the abbot that Merton's popularity was such that hordes of zealous fans might descend on the monastery and ransack the place in search of Merton memorabilia, anything related to the famous monk. He must have imagined Merton fans hiding behind every corner and every bush. He was concerned enough that at some point he appointed Brother Irenaeus, as head of the tailoring shop, the task of collecting and disposing of Thomas Merton's personal possessions. The way it was related to me, Abbot Flavian essentially said, "Just get the stuff out of here. I don't want to know what you do with it all. Just get it out of the monastery." Brother Irenaeus took it to mean that he was to destroy Merton's worldly possessions. Although most of the possessions were gathered from his hermitage, they also included items Merton took with him in his luggage, like the silk ties he had purchased at a haberdashery in Bangkok.

Brother Irenaeus gathered three metal trunks from a storeroom. The trunks had belonged to his brother monks when they first moved to the monastery. There were dozens of them shipped from all over the world. The three he chose had shipping labels from as far away as Rome. He filled the three with things that had belonged to Merton, from his socks and underwear, to religious garments like the white cassock and black scapular he wore in the iconic photograph of him with the Dalai Lama, to his iconic denim jacket with his laundry tag "127" sewn onto the front. And Brother Irenaeus tossed other things into the trunks, Merton's enormous Trappist psalter in French, his ceremonial flagellant (a small leather whip), even his pillows, stained yellow from where his head had lain upon them for so many years. Despite what he thought were the abbot's orders, Brother Irenaeus could not bring himself to destroy the assemblage. Instead, it was decided that he and Sister Mary Pius would safeguard the collection on behalf of their deceased and beloved friend and mentor. Brother Irenaeus loaded the trunks into one of the monastery's jeeps and drove them someplace for temporary safe-keeping.

To the abbot's relief or chagrin, no hordes of souvenir hunters ever stormed the walls of the abbey in search of relics or keepsakes. I sometimes wonder if he ever came to regret his decision to dispose of so many of Merton's belongings. But then, as with himself, every monk at Gethsemani had taken a sacred vow that included poverty. Either way, he must have believed that the objects had been destroyed as he had ordered. As far as I know, he never asked Brother Irenaeus about what he had done with the trunks.

The Abbot's Homily for Thomas Merton

Helen Marie and Robert attended the mass held for Thomas Merton at the Abbey of Gethsemani on December 11, 1968, the day after his death, and both were present at the funeral service and burial six days later on Tuesday, December 17. Robert personally cast a shovelful of soil into the grave of his brother monk, friend, and spiritual teacher. At the Mass, Abbot Flavian Burns read from a prepared two-page homily entitled, "Homily at the Mass for Father M. Louis (Thomas Merton)". In attendance at the somber event were nuns from the Sisters of Loretto, including Sister Mary Pius, and most, if not all, of one hundred twenty-eight or so monks who called Gethsemani home and considered Merton to be their brother.

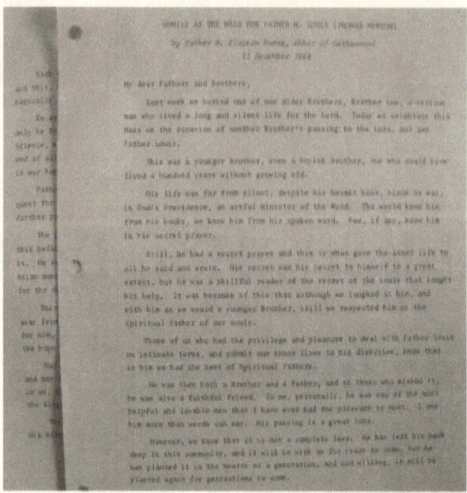

(Abbot Flavian's "Homily at the Mass for Thomas Merton)

In his Homily, Abbot Flavian called Merton "boyish" in the sense that he was someone "who could have lived a hundred years without growing old." He also said that while "the world knew [Merton] from his books, we knew him from his spoken word. Few, if any, knew him in his secret prayer.... Those of us who had the privilege and pleasure to deal with Father Louis on intimate terms, and to submit our inner lives to his direction, know that in him we had the best of Spiritual Fathers."

On hearing this, Sister Mary Pius smiled sadly. She counted herself among the "few" who knew Fr. Louis's secret prayers and deepest self, and she had undertaken an amazing adventure so that she could "submit her inner life" to Father Louis' spiritual guidance. And now he was gone.

A hot tear ran down her cheek.

Abbot Flavian went on to say that before leaving on his "Asian Journey," Fr. Louis had told him in a private conversation that he believed he was going to die during the trip. Abbot Flavian remarked that at first he thought Merton was jesting, but Fr. Louis assured him it was not a joke, that he was serious. But Abbot Flavian did not elaborate further, which must have raised some eyebrows among the audience.

On page two of his Homily, Abbot Flavian specifically addressed what Merton had said to him before he left:

> The possibility of death was not absent from his [Merton's] mind. We spoke of this before he set out—first jokingly, then seriously. He was ready for it. He even saw a certain fittingness in dying over there amidst those Asian monks, who symbolized for him man's ancient and perennial desire for the deep things of God.

The abbot's words struck Helen Marie hard.

What had Father Louis told the abbot, and more importantly, what was the abbot not disclosing about the conversation that had turned "serious"? She wondered if Merton had told the abbot the same thing he had told her that day beside the statue of Joseph. In confidence, Merton had told her his secret and made her to promise never to divulge their conversation to anyone, not even to Brother Irenaeus, with whom she was in love and wanted to marry. But Helen Marie felt that she had to talk to someone. If Fr. Louis' death was not due to natural causes or by accident as the newspapers reported, she had to tell someone. Something had to be done.

The authorities needed to know.

The little nun wrestled with her feelings.

Helen Marie didn't see Brother Irenaeus again until weeks after the Christmas Mass at Gethsemani. She implored Brother Irenaeus to help set up an appointment for her to speak to the abbot. She impressed on him that the matter was urgent and that it was related to Merton's death. She said she "knew certain things that she needed to tell the abbot." Brother Irenaeus was curious, but he was respectful enough not to ask too many questions. It took a while, but a meeting was eventually set sometime in March. Helen Marie would have her chance to speak her mind. At the good Sister's request, Brother Irenaeus was invited to attend.

What came out during the meeting was astonishing and revealing.

Naturally, Abbot Flavian [Burns] knew Sister Mary Pius, as did former Abbot Fox (also known as Father Monk James), who had been Merton's abbot for many years. The abbess at the Sisters of Loretto Motherhouse had communicated with both abbots to ensure that the nun's meetings with Fr. Louis were discreetly chaperoned. It was Flavian, and Fox before him, who had appointed Br. Irenaeus to the task. Only a few months earlier, in September, Brother Irenaeus had met with Abbot Flavian to discuss his desire to leave the order and marry Sister Mary Pius. And it was Flavian who directed Br. Irenaeus to remove Merton's personal belongings from the monastery after his death. Both abbots recognized that Father Louis and the nun had become close friends over the last couple of years.

Officially or unofficially, Merton was her spiritual mentor.

Abbot Flavian and Abbot Fox sat across the table from Sister Mary Pius and Brother Irenaeus, who had informed them that the nun wanted to talk to them about Fr. Louis' death. Abbot Flavian had a folder in front of him while the little nun related the conversation she had had with Fr. Louis just days before he left on his fateful trip, the one by the statue of Joseph. Brother Irenaeus interrupted only to affirm to both abbots that the good Sister had indeed met with Fr.

Louis just as she described, but that he was standing too far away to have overheard what was said.

Sister Mary Pius related to the abbots that Father Louis had told her it was likely that he would not return from his trip. When she asked why he would say something like that, she said, Merton had made her promise never to reveal what he was about to tell her.

Helen Marie took a deep breath before continuing.

She told the abbots and the monk how, there on the knoll in the shadow of the giant statue of Joseph looking down over the monastery named after his blessed wife, Thomas Merton revealed his plan to fulfill Jesus's instruction that his followers must be peacemakers (Matthew 5:9). Helen Marie calmly recounted Merton's plan to sneak out of Thailand after the conference in Bangkok, and to make his way to North Vietnam, where he would surrender himself as a prisoner of war. As a conscientious objector and non-combatant—a hostage for peace—his captivity might help bring about the end of the war by influencing public sentiment against the war back home and abroad.

Helen Marie said she had voiced her fear that he might suffer great hardships, including torture, and that he might even die or be killed. Father Louis replied that it was God's Will. He said he had prayed about it for a long time, and that he was convinced it was the right thing to do. Besides, he said, as a monk he was already used to a life of privation. To assuage her concerns, Merton half-jokingly told her that he would have more time to pray if he were locked up in a cell. Father Louis went on to say that he feared he might be killed *before* setting off for North Vietnam. He reminded her of the strange men he had seen waiting to waylay him along the road to his hermitage. He said from the look of them, they might have been F.B.I.

agents (Helen Marie said Merton had commented about their matching crew cuts). He commented that his new book, *Faith & Violence*, was critical of President Johnson and his administration for their war-mongering in Southeast Asia and for what he saw as an unjust war. He told her that he was convinced the government—the F.B.I. or the C.I.A.—had been intercepting his mail, both coming and going. He was concerned that they knew his itinerary, and that they might be suspicious of his plans. Merton told her that he had sent or was sending out a letter to friends in which he insisted that he had no intention of going anywhere near Vietnam during his travels. He said he'd added the statement to alleviate concerns or suspicions of anyone who might intercept his letter, especially the F.B.I. or C.I.A., so that by throwing them off-track he might accomplish his plan unhindered. Helen Marie was among the friends who received Merton's mimeographed "Farewell Letter" (below).

(Merton's letter to friends before departing on his Asian Journey)

Both abbots listened with great interest. More than once they exchanged knowing glances.

They knew she was telling the truth.

Brother Irenaeus knew that Merton and Sister Mary Pius had spoken before he left, having been their chaperone during the visit, but he had no idea of the gravity of what the two had talked about. Although he had seen the grave expression of worry and the tears on her face afterward, he could not have imagined the deadly seriousness of what Father Louis had told her and the dire ramifications.

He thought it was just a sad goodbye.

When an emotional Sister Mary Pius had finished reciting what Merton had told her, Abbot Flavian replied that Father Louis had told him and Abbot Fox the same thing, namely his plan to surrender himself to the North Vietnamese to help end the war. He had also voiced his concern that agents of the United States government might try to stop him if they had even an inkling of his plan. He had mentioned in particular the C.I.A., which had a robust and unchecked presence in Bangkok during the war in Vietnam.

Sister Mary Pius asked Abbot Flavian why he hadn't said all that in the eulogy at Merton's Mass. In her own words, recollected as best she could remember from that meeting, the abbot replied, "What do you think would happen if news got out that the United States government assassinated a Catholic priest, especially one as famous as Thomas Merton, for trying to bring about peace by hastening the end of an unjust war? There are tens of millions of Catholics in America. A beloved former president was Catholic. Such news could have dire consequences for both the nation and for the Church. Father Louis was aware that what he planned to do was dangerous. He knew he might be killed in an effort to stop him from fulfilling his plan. Both of us [abbots] tried to talk him out of it, but he was adamant. He said he had prayed hard about it, and that he felt certain it was God's Will that he go, even if it meant his death."

Abbot James Fox told Sister Mary Pius and Br. Irenaeus that he'd written a letter to Fr. Louis in October, while he was still in India, before he left for Thailand. He said it worried him that after living so closely in the same abbey for twenty-seven years, he might never get a chance to say goodbye.

Not long before the March 1969 meeting with Abbot Flavian, Sister Mary Pius, and Brother Irenaeus, retired Abbot Fox had written a letter to the Gethsemani Diaspora. In the six-page letter, dated February 1, 1969, the elderly Fox recounted how he learned of Merton's death. Abbot Flavian had sent Br. Patrick (Hart), who was Merton's secretary, along with Br. Lawrence, Abbot Flavian's secretary, to see Abbot Fox at his little hermitage. After arriving in one of the monastery's Jeeps, Br. Patrick told him, "you'd better sit down." It so happened that the day Merton died was also Fox's birthday. Abbot Fox thought the unexpected visit was a ruse to get him to go back to the monastery for a birthday surprise.

"I realized that this day, Dec. 10, was my birthday – and probably they were up to some trick or other to help me celebrate. Perhaps Fr. Flavian had sent [sic] things up with them for a surprise dinner, to have lunch with me. I was bound they wouldn't pull any tricks on me. So I answered: 'Go on — I don't need to sit down.'"

Abbot Fox was unprepared for what Br. Patrick said next.

"Well, OK – The message is this – that Father Louis is dead."

Merton had told the abbot of his concerns about dying before he departed for Asia. Still, believing it was a ruse related to his birthday, Abbot Fox's response was one of incredulity.

"Come now – you certainly have thought up the most improbable and impossible thing. You don't think I am going to swallow that — do you?"

But Br. Patrick and Br. Lawrence said, according to Fox, "Fr. Flavian received a message from the State Department in Washington D. C. Later a phone call all the way from the American Embassy in Bangkok that Fr. Louis had been electrocuted by a faulty wire in a large electric fan in his room. Either that or he had a heart attack and grabed [sic] the fan and it fellwith [sic] him . . ." (Abbot Fox, Personal Letter to the Gethsemani Diaspora, p. 1)

At the end of Abbot Fox's six-page letter to the Diaspora, he included a mimeograph of his two-page letter to Merton dated October 6, 1968, which reads exactly like someone saying goodbye to an old friend or family member who is dying, and as if the author wanted to say his piece before it was too late. In the letter, Abbot Fox speaks of how hard he was on Father Louis at times, but says that he did it out of love and genuine concern for his brother monk's spiritual maturity.

He wrote, "So, in your regard, dear Fr. Louis, I would not be the least surprised, if I have indeed appeared as your 'Bête-noir'—'number one'—your 'nemesis.' But really, no. Such is not the case. You never had, nor never will have one, who has been a more faithful and loyal friend and brother—than myself. I never had any other motive in your regard than your best eternal interests." (Abbot Fox, Personal Letter to Thomas Merton, p. 2)

It is clear in the letter that Abbot Fox knew that Thomas Merton was not going to return to the abbey any time soon, if ever. The fact is Merton's itinerary indicated that he was to return home to Kentucky in less than two months. Abbot Fox could have waited until Merton was home safe and sound to tell him these things in person.

The only reason he would have sent such a letter so close to Merton's scheduled return was that he knew Merton was approaching the time when he would implement his plan to surrender himself to the North Vietnamese. Merton would either die in captivity as a P.O.W. or be imprisoned for an indeterminate time, years possibly, or he would be killed by American agents to stop him from accomplishing his goal. Abbot Fox knew that his letter might be his last chance to communicate with his brother monk.

Merton replied to Abbot Fox's letter on October 20, 1968 from Calcutta. The epistolary exchange shows that, contrary to the way some Merton scholars have portrayed their relationship as contentious, neither Fox nor Merton felt it was so. Merton's response was heartfelt and respectful. In reply, he wrote how they were one another's confessor and that "I never personally resented any of your decisions, because I knew you were following your conscience and the policies that seemed necessary then. He mentions briefly that his travels in Asia had been hard and that he had suffered a "slight case of dysentery." Merton concludes his letter, "Be sure that I have never changed in my respect for you as Abbot, and affections as Father. Our different views certainly did not affect our deep agreement on the real point of life and of our vocation." (Thomas Merton, Personal Letter to Abbot Fr. James Fox, p. 1)

Mimeographed copies of both Abbot Fox's letter to Merton and Merton's response were eventually provided to Brother Irenaeus and Sister Mary Pius, as well as to other members of the Gethsemani Diaspora.

What struck me most about my interviews with Helen Marie was the way in which she clearly remembered these conversations even fifty years later. She swore to their accuracy and truthfulness, so much so that she attested to them in a signed and witnessed affidavit.

Abbot Flavian counselled the little nun never to publicly disclose what Father Louis told her that day, saying that it was better that the world thought Father Louis had died of a heart attack or by freak accident rather than to disclose the alarming possibility. He pointed out that they couldn't prove he was killed anyhow. Certainly none of the reports he had received from Bangkok pointed to murder or conspiracy, though he did acknowledge some inconsistencies in the various reports. Abbot Flavian gave Sister Mary Pius a copy of the letter he had received from the six Trappist-Cistercian delegates at the conference, which mentioned a bloody wound on the back of Father Louis' skull. (The good Sister had seen the letter before, as Brother Irenaeus had shared with her the copy he was given by the abbot on December 19.)

Both abbots thought it preposterous to believe Merton suffered a heart attack. To Abbot Flavian, it seemed clear that someone had killed Merton—most likely with a blow to the back of the head—and then "staged" his death to look accidental. After all, he said, wouldn't previous tenants of the room or the house-cleaning maid have touched the fan? Why hadn't previous tenants "received a fatal shock from standing in bare feet on the stone floor" as the letter from the six Trappists delegates in Bangkok suggested? Why was the fan faulty only at the moment that Thomas Merton touched it? Merton had been staying in the bungalow for days before his death. Surely he had turned it on previously or had moved it or had stood on the stone floor in his bare feet.

Before adjourning the meeting, Abbot Flavian instructed Brother Irenaeus—who was dumbfounded from hearing all of this—not to disclose publicly the nature of their meeting or of the conversation between Father Louis and Sister Mary Pius. For his part, Brother Irenaeus kept his word, taking the story to his grave.

A Nun and a Monk Walk into a Wedding Chapel

In the months before Thomas Merton left on his ill-fated trip to Asia, Sister Mary Pius and Br. Irenaeus often sought Father Louis' counsel about their growing love for each other. Br. Irenaeus even talked to the abbot about it. Increasingly, they wanted to get married, but being a monk and a nun complicated matters, to say the least. Merton counseled them that should they choose to leave their respective monastic orders, both could still serve God as laypeople in different capacities.

"Cloistered monastics don't have a corner on the God market," he said jokingly. "You could be married and still uphold your vows."

Merton had a great sense of humor. Though he could be serious about religion, social justice, war, and his prolific writing, all accounts suggest that he was jovial.

Sister Mary Pius and Brother Irenaeus took Father Louis' words to heart. With their beloved friend and mentor gone, there was nothing left to stop them from getting married.

But fate has a way of getting in the way of plans.

In March of 1969, three months after Thomas Merton was buried, Helen Marie had to go home to take care of her dying mother. She didn't know how long she might be gone, or if she'd ever return to Kentucky. Fearing he might never see her again, Robert wrote her a poem, which he gave to her before she left. Brother Irenaeus begins the poem, entitled "On Leaving an Angel," telling Helen Marie that, "From out of God you came / Piercing my sheltered life," and that she had "enraptured his heart" and "transfigured his soul / with the crystal Christly pureness / of virginity in love." He professes that his love for her is "pure passionless passion / burning cool ... tempered by glacial chasteness."

As it turned out, Helen Marie's mother died within a few months, and she returned to Louisville that summer. But she would no longer live at the Sisters of Loretto Motherhouse in Nerinx. She was no longer a sister in the order of the Sisters Adorers of the Precious Blood. Her request for dispensation had been granted while she was caring for her mother. For the first time since the early 1950s, she was just Helen Marie. The plan was for her to live in Louisville and wait for her future husband to join her. With the help of a letter of recommendation Thomas Merton had given her (see below), Helen Marie got a job as a live-in maid and gardener at the mansion of the Hillerich family, a wealthy old Louisville family that owned the Louisville Slugger baseball bat company. Soon after, Brother Irenaeus—now simply Robert Grimes, having left the Abbey of Gethsemani—also took a job at the mansion as a groundskeeper and handyman. Robert's dispensation from the Abbey probably came months after he left, such is the usual process. Despite being engaged, they boarded in separate bedrooms.

> Jan 13. 67
>
> Whom it may concern.
>
> I am writing this note for Sister Helen Marie who is looking for a simple kind of retired life with a small job temporarily while she is thinking over the next step in her vocation.
>
> I would appreciate if you would help her in this. Gratefully,
>
> Thomas Merton

(Letter of Recommendation by Thomas Merton)

Robert and Helen Marie were married at St. Francis of Assisi Catholic Church on Bardstown Road in Louisville on December 10, 1969, exactly one year to the day after Thomas Merton's death; that way they would remember him on every anniversary they celebrated in the future. Their wedding reception was held at the mansion where they worked and lived. The daughter of the wealthy family was Helen Marie's bridesmaid.

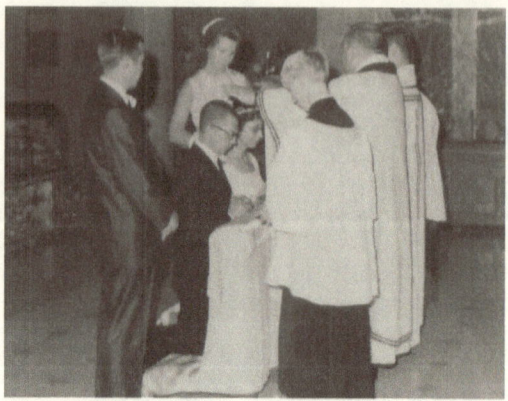

(Helen Marie and Robert getting married at
St. Francis of Assisi Catholic Church in Louisville)

The monks of Gethsemani baked their wedding cake. During a speech to the attendees, they both thanked their departed friend, Father Louis, for his help in bringing them together.

(The bride and groom cutting the wedding cake
made by the monks at Gethsemani)

Helen Marie told me that in their forty years of marriage she and Robert never consummated their union in the carnal sense. A man of his word, Robert kept his promise to cherish and uphold his wife's vows as a celibate nun. It would be almost incredible to believe if it were not for the fact that my friend told me it was true on many occasions. She was adamant. It was apparent at the time she told me that she was a little uncomfortable talking about it, yet a little proud at the same time. I have no reason not to believe her.

(The wedding party outside of St. Francis of Assisi Church)

After the wedding, the newlyweds moved into a house at 1620 NE Rosewood in Louisville, where they lived for the next fifteen years. Thanks to his vocational training at the abbey, Robert got a job working at a local printing company, while Helen Marie worked at various jobs, including as a waitress at a diner where a shifty co-worker strong-armed her into giving him a priceless artifact from the trunks containing Thomas Merton's possessions. It was also during the years in Louisville that Irving Stone got wind of their story and pleaded with them to tell him the story of their friendship with Merton, so he could write about it.

(Helen Marie and Robert Grimes, c. 1970)

In 1985, Helen Marie and Robert moved to Lee's Summit, a sprawling suburb outside Kansas City, Missouri. They bought a nice two-story house with a large yard on a street lined with trees. For the last two decades of their working lives, Helen Marie and Robert worked in the Prayer Room at Unity Village, an extensive interfaith campus sitting on over 1,200 beautiful and serene acres, where they spent their eight-hour shifts praying for people who phoned in requests for prayers or who scribbled prayer requests on notes left in a drop box. Then, as it is today, Unity Village was a mecca of interfaith studies and New Age Spiritualism. Unity Village is the headquarters of Unity Church, which nowadays has over two million followers. The campus has its own printing press and publishes and produces an astonishing array of books and pamphlets on religion, as well as a slick magazine called *Unity*. Today, it has a wonderful bookstore and coffee house well worth visiting.

During those decades at Unity Village, people, especially co-workers, heard Helen Marie and Robert's tale of their friendship with Thomas Merton, and how they had trunks full of his belongings.

A Nun and a Monk Walk into a Wedding Chapel

(Helen Marie and Robert Grimes, c. 2000)

Robert suffered a stroke in 2004, which left him mostly paralyzed. He had to be moved to an assisted living facility. For the next five years, until his death in 2009, Helen Marie spent almost every waking hour at his bedside. She would only go home at night when visiting hours ended. Perhaps it's best to let Helen Marie tell it in her own words. The following is taken verbatim from a letter she sent to friends eulogizing Robert:

> On August 10th of this year (2009), Robert made his transition to the Celestial realms of God's Pure Love and Light. As you probably already know, he had been in a nursing home since the end of December 2004 as a result of a massive stroke caused by a blood clot on the right side of his brain, leaving him completely paralyzed on the entire left side of his body. He was not expected to live out the week, and I was advised by his physicians to get his affairs in order, make funeral arrangements, and call his immedi-

ate family if they wished to see him alive for the last time, which I did. Within a week, Robert's condition began to improve and he survived nearly five years beyond their grim prognosis.

On the day of Robert's stroke, I retired permanently from my position at Unity Village after having worked for twenty years in the Telephone Prayer Ministry, which I loved, so as to care for Robert at a nursing home not far from our home. I went there seven days a week making sure he was not neglected in any way, since most nursing homes are understaffed . . . I worked with him every way I could, emotionally, physically, and spiritually, as a whole person, and my darling Robert was more than grateful. He once told me during one of our spiritual discussions that he considered having a stroke a blessing in disguise because it stopped his ego in its tracks and completely transformed his life inwardly into a new man in Christ. His intimacy with God through prayer, and an awareness of his Oneness with God, became the most important and beautiful occupation in his life. Robert became a living, shining example of loving kindness and patience, and he expressed gratitude to everyone assisting him, even for the smallest service rendered to him. He was genuinely loved by all, including the many physicians that treated him in and out of hospitals throughout his many setbacks. Oftentimes, the doctors expressed their deep admiration for his wonderful attitude and outlook and hoped that one day they too would follow his beautiful and powerful example.

I considered it to be a great honor and privilege to have

been with him, caring for him, loving him, and supporting him throughout these challenging and difficult years. My dear, sweet husband never complained about anything . . . Although I miss his presence so very much and the tears still flow at times, I would never want him back in that sick and paralyzed body. He died from pneumonia that he contracted during one of his hospital stays, which never left him, together with a fatal urinary infection, caused by his catheter that poisoned his entire system and finally shut his body down.

My Robert had a beautiful passing and was not fearful of dying, especially since he had a near death experience the year before and had actually visited the other side of the veil. He told me how gloriously beautiful it was. He also told me that he heard my prayers to the Holy Spirit and began to follow my voice back into his body as the paramedics began working on him before taking him to the hospital. While he was on the other side, he had encountered beautiful Beings of Light and was told by them that it was not his time to remain there, and that he had much more love to give and to receive.

As my husband was dying, I placed my head next to his on the pillow and whispered in his ear how much I loved him and how grateful I was for our forty-one years of marriage. I asked his forgiveness for anything I had ever done that hurt him, and then I gave him my blessing to leave this world with the promise that I would see him again someday. Moments later, my beloved Robert's beautiful spirit was finally set free, never to suffer and die again.

Robert's remains were buried at the Higginsville Missouri

State Veteran's Cemetery, about forty miles east of Kansas City. The stone marker reads: "Robert A. Grimes, WWII, Staff Sergeant, Ex-POW, Purple Heart." I was surprised to read that he had received the Purple Heart medal. Robert had never mentioned it to me in all our many years together. But I suspect that he received it for wounds he suffered from German bayonets during the infamous "Death March" to Stalag Luft IV when he was a POW in WWII.

(Photo by Carita Trent, 2021; used with permission)

Many of you may have never known this, but Robert was a sensitive and gifted writer. Throughout his lifetime, when his spirit moved him to write, he would put his thoughts down on paper. He wrote about people he met and who had touched him in some unique way, and he especially wrote about his experiences during World War II.

He also composed poems. In fact, during his many years at the Abbey of Gethsemani monastery where Robert was a monk for seventeen years, Robert often showed his poems to his brother monk, Father Louis, and asked for feedback as Fr. Louis was a famous poet and writer known to the rest of the world as Thomas Merton.

I would like to close this eulogy and share with you a particular poem Robert wrote for me in March of 1969, after I left Kentucky to go back to New Jersey to help care for my mother who was dying. I was uncertain if or when I'd ever return to Kentucky. Thinking he might never see me again, Robert wrote a poem for me entitled "On Leaving an Angel," which reads in part:

> For He Who gave now takes away
> And blessed be His name.
> The beauty, love and joy you gave,
> I gave,
> Though in a lesser quality,
> Yet, drop for drop.
> The fusion then is now, complete.
> Through mystic union
> Born of God
> We have become each other's
> Sacrament.
> And shall I mourn your leaving?
> How can you leave
> When you are me?
> And can the breath be severed
> From the breathing?
> Or the heart its beating?

> I rejoice in our eternal oneness.
> You in me and I in you
> And we in His Divinity,
> Through time and space our bodies may
> Divide,
> Who cares?
> The passion of our Christocentric love
> Will rise and grow
> Until,
> In the madness of his swirling flood-tide
> We be caught,
> Swept up, engulfed,
> In the loving Trinitarian embrace,
> Where day shall know no evening
> And love no end.

Robert's poem has been etched deep within my heart and soul for forty years. Now that he has left me, and I am uncertain when I will see him again, I now apply the message of the poem to him. With these profound and soul-stirring words from Robert's poem, I leave you with my heart's overflowing love, gratitude, and prayers that God will be the most important, beautiful, real thing in each of your lives and those of your loved ones as well. May your whole being be gladdened as you recognize and awaken to the presence of God abundantly within, around and about you, to bring forth miracles of blessings beyond your greatest dreams, aspirations, and expectations.

Life is never taken away, only changed as we go from Life to Life. We are just changing garments. There is no death in the pathway of Life and Love, only ongoing Life, for the spirit is eternal and immortal. I love you all most dearly."

–HMG

The Pilfering of the Thomas Merton Collection (1970-2015)

Helen Marie is so kind, so innocent and naive, that she couldn't keep a secret. She was proud of her friendship with Thomas Merton, and she was equally proud to let others know that she had been friends with the famous monk, and that she and her husband, former Brother Irenaeus, were safekeeping trunks full of Merton's possessions. From the beginning, after the two moved to Louisville, family, friends, and colleagues wanted a piece of Thomas Merton for themselves. Some begged, some bullied, and some stole. Over the years, piece by piece, the Thomas Merton collection was diminished. While some of the pilfered objects eventually made their way to the Thomas Merton Center at Bellarmine University in Louisville or to the Thomas Merton Center in Pittsburgh, a few artifacts were never seen again. Of the objects that were donated, the donors failed to mention who was the rightful owner of the objects, seeking only to connect their names with Merton's. Each story of the pilfering of the collection deserves to be told, for each illuminates a sad, even pathetic, but very human, rationale. One of our greatest weaknesses is our capacity to rationalize even our worst behavior.

One of the first pilferings was by a nun, which, in many ways, makes perfect sense. Sister T. was one of Helen Marie's fellow nuns back at The Sister Adorers of the Precious Blood in Brooklyn. The two had been close during Helen Marie's thirteen years there as a nun. After Robert and Helen Marie married and moved to Louisville, Sister T. came to stay with them for a visit. Like many of the young nuns back at Precious Blood, Sister T. adored Thomas Merton. She had been one of the nuns secretly reading Merton's books. When Helen Marie showed her friend the trunks full of Merton's belongings, the nun became fixated on possessing some of the objects. Day after day, she implored Helen Marie to give her something of Merton's to cherish.

Because of this persistence, before Sister T. returned to her convent, Helen Marie gave her Merton's Cistercian rosary, two of his coarse and ragged fieldwork shirts, and one of his white tee-shirts. The rosary was significant. Over twenty-seven years, Merton had said a million prayers while thumbing the worn, black wooden beads. Sister T. told Helen Marie that she planned to be buried with the rosary. Helen Marie didn't really want to give it up—not out of possessiveness, but out of love for Merton. But Sister T. was relentless. Day after day, she asked to be given the rosary, to take with her back to the Brooklyn convent, the place where Helen Marie as Sister Mary Pius had prayed and toiled for years. Eventually, Helen Marie complied. Years later, Sister T. moved to another monastery. In 1993, she sent a letter to Helen Marie and Robert. In the two-page letter, she mentioned Merton, and remembered the time she'd stayed at the Grimes house in Louisville, in 1970.

In the summer of 2015, Helen Marie asked me to track down Sister T. and to ask if she would return the objects so that they could be donated to museums with the rest of the collection. It had been years since the two had communicated. Helen Marie instructed me to begin by contacting the convent in Brooklyn, even though it had been half a century since she had left the protected confines of their vine-covered walls. Sister T. was no longer living there. By chance, a retired priest happened to hear about my inquiry and contacted me. He remembered her, and gave me contact information for the convalescent home for retired nuns where Sister T. was living. I sent her a letter, describing how I was writing on behalf of her old friend Helen Marie, formerly Sister Mary Pius, who was collaborating with me to donate Thomas Merton's artifacts to museums. I wrote that Helen Marie remembered giving certain objects to her back around 1970, and we wondered if she still had them, and if she did, would she kindly send them to me. She wrote back and included her telephone number. We spoke on the phone several times after that. She eventually sent me a box with a couple of Merton's work shirts from Gethsemani, but when I asked about the black rosary, she concocted a story.

"It's in my room somewhere," she'd say. "It must be in a box. Gracious! I know it's around here someplace."

This went on for months.

In the end, she never did send it.

I suspect she will get or has gotten her wish to be buried with Thomas Merton's rosary.

Later, with her health failing, the retired Sister T. found another artifact she had been given, one of Merton's white T-shirts, torn and crudely mended by Merton himself. Like all the pieces of clothing, the T-shirt had a faded 127 handwritten in black ink on the collar.

It smelled musty, as if it had been stored in a box for fifty years. If you ask me, it may be the T-shirt that is visible in the iconic photo of Merton standing outside his hermitage wearing the blue denim jacket (see below). Helen and I agreed to send the T-shirt to Paul Pearson at the Thomas Merton Center at Bellarmine University to accurately complete the ensemble.

(Thomas Merton in his blue denim jacket, blue denim work shirt, and white T-shirt; c. 1968)

Not long after Sister T.'s visit, Helen Marie applied for a job working as a waitress in a diner in Louisville. When the manager asked if she had experience, Helen Marie smiled and said that she did. After all, she thought, back at the convent she had been a scullery maid working in the kitchen doing much the same kind of work—setting tables at meal time, bringing out the food, and then cleaning up and washing dishes afterward. The difference is her sister nuns didn't order off a menu. No "I want whole wheat toast, lightly browned, and I want my eggs over easy."

The manager figured out pretty quickly that Helen Marie didn't have any real waitressing experience, but he kept her nonetheless. After all, she was trustworthy, friendly, punctual, and hardworking.

One day, there was an article about Thomas Merton in the local newspaper that talked about how famous he was. Helen Marie recalls it was on the anniversary of his death. She casually mentioned how she knew Merton and how she and her husband had all this stuff that had belonged to him. Her boss, a big, fat, greasy-as-fried-eggs man, saw an opportunity.

It's important to remember that in the late 1960s to early 1970s, women had little agency regarding workplace harassment. It was a time when waitresses still had their rear ends pinched or patted by lecherous men as they walked by. They were taken advantage of by their male bosses with little or no recourse. Helen Marie's boss browbeat and bullied her into giving him an artifact from the collection, not because he admired Merton or had ever read a single word of his writing, but because he saw how famous Merton was, and he wanted his fifteen minutes of fame.

Helen Marie felt that if she didn't give in to his demand she would be fired. She needed the job. She and Robert were struggling to build a new life together. They had a house to pay for. But at the same time, she didn't want to part with anything that had belonged to her dear, dead friend. She cried about the intimidation and prayed for guidance. In the end, with little choice in the matter, she reluctantly gave her boss the academic hood that Merton had received when the University of Kentucky awarded him an honorary doctorate in 1967, Merton's only honorary degree.

Shortly thereafter, the greasy con man contacted the newspapers and concocted some story of how he had come to have this amazing historical object that had once belonged to Thomas Merton, and concluded that out of benevolence he was donating it to then-Bellarmine College. University of Kentucky officials verified that the hood as authentic. He made it sound like he knew Merton personally. He never mentioned Helen Marie or her husband.

To prove what she told me, Helen Marie gave me a handwritten note from Thomas Merton. The note was given to Brother Irenaeus, her husband, shortly after Merton received the honorary doctoral hood. It read: "Dear Br. Irenaeus This useless object belongs with a degree I got. I suppose it ought to be kept someplace?? Anyway, if you have a corner to store it away, I would be grateful. Thanks in Jesus br m [brother monk] Louis" Something like a PS clarifies: "of recent date, so that's how I come to have it around."

The note has since been donated to the Thomas Merton Center archival collection.

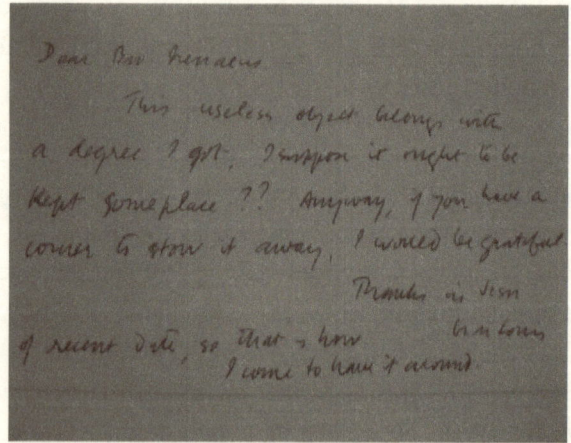

(Merton's 1967 note to Br. Irenaeus)

It really troubled Helen Marie when she saw the hood displayed in the Thomas Merton Center with her old boss's name attached to it as the donor. She talked about it for the rest of the trip back to Missouri. Finally, unable to bear the insult, Helen Marie implored me to contact Paul Pearson and tell him the truth, and ask him to correct the lie.

I sought advice from two of Merton's old friends, James W. Douglass and Fr. Matthew Fox, both of whom are prolific writers whom I admire greatly. Both agreed that it was time to right an old wrong. So, in early 2018, I contacted Dr. Pearson and told him the true story of how the artifact came to be in the museum's collection, and requested that the provenance of the object be rightfully acknowledged as having been donated by Helen Marie and Robert Grimes, or at the very least as part of the Grimes-Smelcer Thomas Merton Collection. As far as I know, the academic hood still bears the name of Helen Marie's old, selfish boss who robbed her of it through bullying and harassment. In the end, he got what he wanted—for his name to be associated with Merton's for all time. It was one of my regrettable failures in representing Helen Marie's wishes regarding the Merton Collection.

The next person who pilfered objects from the trunks was Robert's own sister. Her story is very much like the one above. On hearing that her brother and sister-in-law had all of these items that had once belonged to Thomas Merton, she talked her brother out of a number of objects, including clothing, notes, photographs, and even a book that Merton's poetry publisher, James Laughlin, founder of New Directions, had inscribed for him. In September of 2009, one month after her brother's death, she finally donated the objects to the Thomas Merton Center at Bellarmine University in Louisville. She also donated Merton's long white religious robe (seen below) to the Thomas Merton Center in Pittsburgh, where she lived. In the summer of 2015, the director there told me that the important artifact is not on display for the public. For a decade, it has sat in a box in a closet.

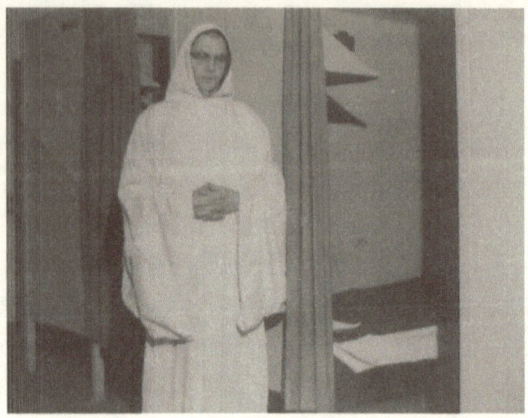

(Br. Irenaeus wearing his robe beside his sleeping alcove,
the same as Thomas Merton would have worn, 1957)

When I reminded the director that many sports fans frame autographed jerseys to hang on their walls as art, she replied they had no money for that. I asked a local frame shop how much it would cost to frame such an item. They estimated less than $200, and that included museum quality glass to protect the artifact from deterioration caused by exposure to sunlight.

Two hundred bucks.

It astounded me that in all those years they hadn't requested donations to cover the cost of framing one of Thomas Merton's religious garments to showcase in the Center. The artifact may as well still be crammed in one of the old trunks in Helen Marie's garage. Helen Marie was insistent that objects from the collection be displayed where people who have been touched by her old friend and teacher could see them safely protected behind glass. At first, Helen Marie had wanted us to donate a few artifacts to the Thomas Merton Center in Pittsburgh. But when I told her what the director had said to me about the robe her sister-in-law had given them, she insisted that we not send them anything from the collection because it was important to her that the objects be displayed publicly.

Like the boss at the diner who only wanted to connect his name to Merton's out of ego, the Agreement to donate the objects to the Thomas Merton Center at Bellarmine University made no mention of their provenance. Robert's sister failed to mention that they came from her brother, who had been one of Merton's brother monks at the Abbey of Gethsemani for two decades, and from his wife of forty years, a former nun who had been Merton's close friend and confidant. In fact, when I met Paul Pearson in Louisville in the summer of 2015 (it was Pearson who signed the Agreement to receive the objects from Robert's sister; I have a copy), it was apparent that Robert's sister never mentioned to him the story of the former monk who married the former nun and how they had come to have the Merton artifacts. Had she mentioned it, Pearson would have responded differently when I "bounced" into his office that summer day. He would have told me that he had heard something about the couple and their treasure trove of Mertonalia. Instead, only her name appears on the Agreement and on the objects donated to the Merton Center. The same was true of the director at the Thomas Merton Center in Pittsburgh. She had no idea that the artifact(s) came from a collection of a former monk and a former nun who had been safeguarding them since Merton's death.

One of the most fascinating stories happened sometime in the late 1970s when Irving Stone came to Louisville to meet Helen Marie and Robert. Stone was the author of a number of biographical novels of historical figures, especially Catholic figures, such as Michelangelo. *The Agony and the Ecstasy* (1961) tells the story of his painting the ceiling of the Sistine Chapel. The book was made into a motion picture in 1965 starring Charleton Heston and Rex Harrison, who starred in *Doctor Doolittle* (1964) and in *My Fair Lady* opposite Audrey Hepburn (1967). Stone also wrote *Lust for Life* (1934), about the life and death of Vincent Van Gogh, which was adapted into a film in 1956. Stone had somehow heard about the Grimes' connection to Thomas Merton and about their amazing collection of artifacts. (Don't ask me how.) Perhaps someone contacted Stone thinking he might want to interview the former monk and nun; based on his previous interests in controversial historical and religious figures, Stone might have been intrigued about writing a book about Thomas Merton and his mysterious death.

But Stone wasn't the first famous writer or director to be interested in the story of Thomas Merton. Years before, Cecil B. DeMille (*The Ten Commandments, Cleopatra, The War of the Worlds*), considered the most commercially successful producer-director in history, wanted to make a motion picture based on *The Seven Storey Mountain*. Merton's reaction was one of terror. He ran to the Abbot to find out how they could put a stop to it, which subsequently led to a clause in Merton's will forbidding his publishers to allow his work to be filmed in any way.

That order still stands today.

Helen Marie and Robert showed Stone the trunks full of Merton's belongings. Stone asked if he could keep the iconic blue denim jacket or the white cassock and black scapular that Merton wore when he visited the Dalai Lama in India, but they said no. Stone asked if he could write about their story, but they weren't ready to tell their story publicly. Unable to convince them otherwise, Stone returned to California empty-handed. He died a decade later in the summer of 1989. Helen Marie says that the reason she and Robert denied Stone their story was because too many of the people involved in the story were still alive. After all, at the time, Merton had only been dead for a little over a decade. In an interview on April 24, 2018, Helen Marie told me and two witnesses, "It wasn't the right time back then. Now is the acceptable time."

I'm thankful that I came along at the acceptable time, and I'm also a little prideful that I scooped the story from Irving Stone.

When I related this story to Paul Pearson, Director of the Thomas Merton Center, his response was skeptical. He said he had never heard of this story. He wondered if Helen Marie was confusing Irving Stone with Cecil B. DeMille's desire to make a motion picture of *The Seven Storey Mountain*. But I reminded him that he could not possibly have known of the Stone story. It had happened to Helen Marie and her husband ten years after they left their respective orders. They had never *publicized* the fact that they had Thomas Merton's worldly possessions stored in trunks in their house in Louisville. That fact didn't become widely known until I'd encountered Helen Marie in the spring of 2015, more than thirty-five years after Stone's request. When Helen Marie first told me the story, I asked if she remembered the author's name. She said it was Robert who mostly spoke with Stone, but she remembered his films, specifically naming the movie with Charleton Heston as Michelangelo and the one about Vincent Van Gogh. When I mentioned Irving Stone (I had read his book on Van Gogh as an undergraduate), she exclaimed, "That's him! He's the one who came to see us." As a follow up to Pearson's concern, I asked Helen Marie if she had meant DeMille, reciting his failed effort to make a motion picture of *The Seven Storey Mountain*. It was clear to me from her response that she had never heard of DeMille's plan to make a movie of Merton's book.

To corroborate Helen Marie's account, I reached out to Stone's estate and family, asking if they knew anything about the story, but I never received a reply one way or the other.

I have no reason to disbelieve Helen Marie.

Besides, a letter from Br. Benedict to John Howard Griffin, Merton's biographer, in the fall of 1971 indicates that folks at Gethsemani were still talking about Helen Marie and Brother Irenaeus two years after they married and moved away (see chapter "Enacting Love"). Perhaps someone mentioned something to Irving Stone or to someone connected to him.

The point of telling these three vignettes is not to ridicule or shame these individuals (all of whom are dead), but to reveal the very human and selfish desire to connect our names to history—for our lives to have mattered and to be remembered. Everyone wants to be famous, even if it lasts for only fifteen minutes as Andy Warhol famously said. The vignettes dispel any notion that safeguarding Thomas Merton's worldly possessions was as simple as hiding them in trunks in a basement or garage. For five decades, Helen Marie and her husband were hounded by requests and demands from family, friends, writers, and co-workers to give up artifacts from the collection. In the process, the contents that once filled three trunks were reduced to two. For half a century, the former monk and former nun bore witness to the greed and vanity of humanity.

The Right Place at the Right Time

Like many writers, I spend a good deal of time sitting in coffee houses. But in the little Midwestern town where I live, such establishments don't seem to last too long. In 2015, I was doing my writing in a booth in the cafeteria of our local grocery store because it was about the only place left in town. The ambiance was far from what I loved about a great coffee house. Still, every morning, like clockwork, I spent an hour or two sitting in my booth—always the same one. Folks used to joke that there should be a sign that said, "Reserved for John Smelcer."

One day toward the end of spring, I was working on a book that was partially influenced by the writings of Thomas Merton. One of his books lay face-up on the table. A gentleman I knew named Jon Waddington stopped by to say hello. Our daughters attended the same preschool. He asked about the book. I told him about my current writing project and how I had been reading Merton. To be honest, I didn't think he'd know who Merton was, but to my great surprise he replied that not only did he know who he was, but he quite matter-of-factly stated that he used to know a former nun who was a close friend of Merton.

Jon continued, telling me how back around the late 1980s and early 90s, he worked as a groundskeeper mowing the vast green lawns at Unity Village, a religious campus outside Kansas City, and about a three-and-a-half hour drive from where we were sitting. He said that his mother, a Unity minister, had been friends with the nun, who worked at Unity Village with her husband back in those days. He said she used to have all these objects that had belonged to Merton. He said he had seen some of them once.

My jaw must have fallen in astonishment.

"More, tell me more," I pleaded.

Briefly, he related what he remembered.

"It was twenty-five years ago," he first reminded me before relating what he could recall.

The way he remembered it, he thought the former nun had once lived near where Merton lived, and they had become friends during the last years of Merton's life. Jon didn't know for sure how she ended up with all the materials, but he remembered that she was married to a former monk from the monastery and that they ended up in Lee's Summit.

I knew enough about Merton to realize that I'd never heard anything about this. This could be important if it was true. A thousand questions went through my mind.

Was she still alive? Did she still live in Lee's Summit? Did she still have the materials? Why hadn't she donated the objects to museums?

Trying to hide my excitement, I asked Jon to find out if she was still alive, and if she was, could he help arrange for me to meet her.

The Right Place at the Right Time

He said he thought his mother might be able to help. He believed she still kept in touch with the former nun. He promised to call her.

It took a couple weeks, but Jon's mother, Jane, helped to arrange a meeting with the former nun at her house in late June. Jon Waddington accompanied me on that first visit. I was excited and anxious on the long drive to Kansas City. My mind was full of questions and doubts. I wondered whether or not the former nun still had the materials. If she did, I wondered if she would show them to me. I pondered how I would recognize whether the artifacts had belonged to Merton or not. I worried that in her mid-eighties, the former nun might suffer from Alzheimer's or dementia and wouldn't be able to tell me anything about the origins of the materials ... if they existed at all. Finally, I wondered if this was all just a wild goose chase.

We arrived at her house on schedule around noon.

I was immediately struck by Helen Marie. She is only a little over five feet tall and weighs around eighty-five pounds. Despite her age, she was so vibrant and exuberant. She welcomed us into her home and we sat down in her living room, which was decorated with porcelain angels, pictures of angels, angel dolls, and collectible plates with images of angels, and Christmas decorations shaped like angels. The windows were covered with blue Styrofoam to help keep the house cool in the summer and warm in the winter. Even the sliding door in the dining room was covered. There must have been hundreds of angels in the dark room. Above the fireplace, which looked as if it hadn't been used in a decade, was a giant framed picture of Jesus.

I introduced myself as a writer, university professor, as an archaeologist, oral historian, as a fellow Catholic, and, like Merton, a student of world religions, and as someone who was trained by the Smithsonian Institution in the proper care of museum artifacts. Most importantly, I let her know that I was familiar with the works of Thomas Merton and that I admired him greatly. I related that I was currently writing a book inspired by him, and that our lives had some striking similarities.

For the next couple of hours, Helen Marie told us how she came to know Thomas Merton. She told us her story about how she was a nun in Brooklyn and how she went to meet Merton and how she later moved to a convent near Merton and how he became her spiritual teacher up until his death on December 10, 1968. She told us about her husband, who had been a brother monk at the Abbey of Gethsemani during most of the years Merton had been there. She related the story of Merton's death and how the Abbot ordered her then-monk husband to round up Merton's possessions and to get rid of them out of fear of relic hunters descending on the monastery in search of souvenirs. She also told us that her husband had died in 2009 and she's been alone ever since. I remember she wept on speaking about Robert's death. I remember, too, that I consoled her with a hug. To verify her story, she brought out photos, as well as notes and letters from Merton. On one of her end tables was a framed black and white photo of her husband during the years he lived as a monk at Gethsemani. I recognized the Trappist attire immediately: the white cassock, the long black scapular, and the long, wide leather belt. To my great delight, her story was checking out. Ever the oral historian, I busily scribbled notes on a yellow legal pad and asked clarifying questions.

I think Helen Marie was impressed by my knowledge of Merton and by my ardent enthusiasm.

At least three times during the interview, I asked Helen Marie if she still had the materials. I remember saying, "You know if you still have the boxes in a basement or in the attic or somewhere, I'd be glad to carry them into the living room for you so we can look at them. It wouldn't be a problem. I'd be glad to do it."

Each time she seemed to ignore my question. But after a while, she came to realize that my interest was sincere. She led us into her garage and pointed at two large trunks buried behind a mountain of boxes. I estimated there were thirty or more boxes. It took a while to move them all out of the way so that we could drag the two trunks to where we could open them.

Both metal trunks looked to be the appropriate age. I had one just like them to store my toys in when I was a boy in the late 60s. Both bore stickers of the places they had been shipped, such as Baltimore and Rome. The Rome stickers immediately caught my attention. After all, the seat of Catholicism, the Vatican, is in Rome. It made sense that Catholic priests might have traveled there at one time or the other. Smaller stamps adorned the outside of the trunks as well. Both were labelled with the same mailing address: Trappist Abbey, Kentucky. All indications were that these trunks were genuine and that they authenticated Helen Marie's amazing story.

I asked how she had the trunks.

She replied that every monk moving to the Abbey was given a list of things they could bring with them. Needless to say, it was a short list. She said it was her husband's job at the Abbey to store the trunks in case they were needed in the future should a man decide to give up life as a monk. She said monks often came and went. Some just needed time to straighten out their minds. When the Abbot ordered Br. Irenaeus to gather Merton's worldly possessions and to get rid of them, Br. Irenaeus took three trunks from a storage room and filled them with Merton's stuff.

I was curious about what had happened to the third trunk. Did she still have it?

I was astounded when she opened the lids. There was an array of objects, from the sweat-stained pillows removed from Merton's narrow bed in his hermitage to his socks and boxer shorts. There was his heavy, oversized Cistercian Psalter (hymn book) from the late 1800s, and his leather flagellant whip (also called a discipline), which I later learned was mostly ceremonial, out of a long tradition of penance and suffering in the Catholic faith (even Teresa of Avila had one). There was his religious clothing, including his white cassock and black scapular that appeared on so many book covers. There were blue denim jackets, blue denim work shirts, blue coarse-fabric shirts worn to stay warm in winter. Wearing coarse, simple, uncomfortable clothing is a sign of austerity in many religions (for instance, the word "Sufi" comes from the coarse clothing they wore), and even tee-shirts. There were three narrow silk suit ties made in Thailand. Almost every piece of clothing had a white square piece of fabric sewn into the cloth with the number "127" written in ink on it. In a few instances, previous numbers had been crossed out and a new number written beneath it. On one of the denim jackets, there were three numbers: two crossed out leaving only the "127" at the bottom. Most of the clothing—especially the work clothes—was worn ragged, patched, unevenly stitched and threadbare in places. They were testament to the fact that for all his fame as one of the world's most famous monks and as the author of a million-selling book (hailed as one of the 100 most important books of the Twentieth Century), Thomas Merton—like Jesus and his wandering Disciples—walked the walk; he lived his life simply, austerely, and in poverty.

(Jon Waddington, the author, and Helen Marie)

Helen Marie told me that for years she had been praying to Thomas Merton to send someone to help her. She didn't have a computer. She didn't know how to use the Internet. Even if she wanted to donate the materials, she had no idea what to do or where to start. She said that she worried that if she died, the trunks full of Merton materials would most likely be tossed into the landfill as musty old junk kept for decades by an elderly hoarder. She prayed for someone to come along who recognized the importance of the collection and who had the wherewithal and capability to help her to donate the materials to museums. She prayed for someone to come along who could tell her story to the world, not for her own edification, but because she wanted Merton's story to be told. She had things to tell the world about Merton. Above all, she prayed for a sign that she would recognize the person for his or her integrity and for a mutual adoration of Merton. She told me that she saw all this in me. She said I even reminded her of Merton, especially when I laughed. In fact, at the time I was the same age Merton was when he died.

She said I was the one she had prayed for.

She hugged me and said that Thomas Merton had sent me to her. I remember her looking up to the sky, clasping her hands together, and saying aloud, "Thank you, Father Louis!"

She told me to take the trunks and to find their proper homes. She trusted me—a virtual stranger she had only known for a couple of hours—with the treasure of her beloved friend's belongings, which she and her husband had safeguarded from almost fifty years. I promised to do right by her and by Merton. I promised to donate all the items to appropriate institutions and to work directly with her in the process, ensuring that she and her late husband received the credit they deserved (not that any of that mattered to Helen Marie; her desire for the artifacts to find safe homes was selfless and without ego). She agreed to meet me regularly in the future so that I could continue to interview her about her friendship with Merton, and write a book about it. As a writer, I promised to tell her story faithfully.

Helen Marie was true to her word. We met dozens of times over the ensuing years.

Eventually, most of the artifacts were donated to the Thomas Merton Center at Bellarmine University in Louisville, Kentucky, where, during his last years of life, Merton himself had collaborated with then-Bellarmine College to establish a center where his materials would be archived and preserved for posterity. At Helen Marie's insistence that the collection be split up a little, in the unlikely event that one place might be destroyed by fire or flood or other peril, some of the artifacts were donated to the Smithsonian Institution's Museum of American History and some to the Vatican.

The Naysayers

The day after I brought Merton's possessions home, I pulled everything out of the metal trunks and took inventory, carefully laying out the artifacts, cataloging and photographing them. Think what you will, but I even tried on some of his clothing. I wore them in arrangements mirroring photographs of him: his denim jeans, white tee-shirt, blue work shirt, blue denim jacket, and navy blue cap. The cap still had strands of his short gray hair inside. I even tried on his religious vestments, including the white cassock and black scapular he wore when he met the Dalai Lama in northern India in late 1968. I can say from the experience that Merton was about two or three inches taller than I am and outweighed me by about twenty-five to thirty pounds.

(The author in Merton's iconic denim jacket, shirt, and jeans; even the white tee-shirt and Navy blue cap was Merton's)

(The author in Merton's cassock and scapular; the one he wore in the iconic photograph with the Dalai Lama in 1968)

The Naysayers

I was so thrilled about the success of my visit with the former nun that I wanted to tell someone who would appreciate the news. As Paul Pearson described me in his foreword, I was "wired with excitement and anticipation."

The first person I called was one of my long-time clergy friends, a Catholic priest back in Alaska. Fr. Leo Walsh is the Judicial Vicar for the Diocese of Anchorage. We had been friends for years. We are similarly aged. Both of us are avid outdoorsmen. We both love dogs. We both grew up in Alaska. We both have advanced degrees. Fr. Leo earned a J.C.L. (doctor of canon law) and a S.T.D. (doctor of sacred theology) from the University of St. Thomas Aquinas in Rome, for which I edited his dissertation. You can imagine the good-natured ribbing I gave him over abbreviation of his degree: "How's your S.T.D. coming along? Taking anything for it?" Fr. Leo is one of the most remarkable people I have ever known. Aside from his extraordinary education, he is a licensed Rugby referee and a private pilot with multiple ratings. During one of our weekly dinners together—the main course was generally some Alaskan game meat, including salmon, halibut, moose, caribou, bison, and even musk ox—he once told me that I was the most Jesus-like person he knew. I don't know if what he said was true, but his words have stuck in my mind all these years. Fr. Leo helped me through the most difficult time of my life. I will always be thankful for his presence during that dismal and hopeless period. Later, when he himself was feeling despondent, I wrote him a letter encouraging him and telling him that he was my role model for what it means to be a good man. I know for a fact that my letter comforted him. I figured if anyone I knew would appreciate my "discovery" it would be him.

We were such close friends, that twice while Fr. Leo was assigned as Associate Director of the Secretariat for Ecumenical and Interreligious Affairs at the United States Conference of Catholic Bishops in Washington D.C., I visited him, staying at the Conference's Staff House. I vividly remember the beautiful campus nestled in a park-like setting right in the heart of Washington D.C. One night we went to a Brazilian restaurant called Fogo de Chão. That night we enjoyed a fantastic—and really expensive—dinner consisting mostly of meat, meat, and more meat. I know how much it cost because I had agreed to treat for dinner since he was putting me up at the Staff House. I recall a waiter coming around with a booze cart asking if we wanted to buy a shot of the liquor he was peddling. Fortunately, I asked how much it would cost before agreeing to buy us both one. I was astounded when the waiter replied that it would cost something like fifty dollars a shot. I looked at the bottle and did the math, calculating how much a full bottle must cost. We passed on the liquor.

After dinner, we'd sit on the roof of the Staff House telling tall stories of our hunting and fishing prowess while smoking cigars and drinking good whiskey and looking out over the city lights. Inevitably, one of us would proclaim some variation of "Fish fear me and tremble at the sound of my name," and we'd both laugh. A few years afterward, I got to meet Archbishop Kurtz, the President of the U. S. Conference of Catholic Bishops. Archbishop Kurtz, like many Catholic leaders nowadays, praised Merton. In fact, he spoke glowingly about Merton at the Frazier Museum in Louisville, Kentucky when artifacts from Helen Marie's Merton collection were first exhibited to the public in late January of 2016.

The Naysayers

(the author wearing a tie that Merton bought in Bangkok,
Helen Marie and Archbishop Kurtz at the Frazier Museum;
Photo courtesy of Dan Johnson)

Fr. Leo's response on hearing about my Thomas Merton "discovery" was unexpected. Despite our similarities, Fr. Leo had a very different perspective when it came to Thomas Merton. He urged me to destroy all of Merton's possessions. Specifically, he said I should drag it all down to my field and dowse the pile in gasoline and set them afire. I was stunned. I asked why he would say such a thing. He was really the first person I had encountered who saw Merton's lifework as anti-Catholic, despite the fact that, like himself, Merton was an ordained Catholic priest. More than that, at the time of his death in 1968, Merton was arguably the most famous monk in the world, Christian or otherwise.

Fr. Leo went on to describe the way some conservative American Catholics have long viewed Merton as a heretic. As he spoke, I had visions of Inquisitions, torture, and witch burnings. The more I listened, the more my heart sank. Here was a friend I admired, respected, and loved telling me that many Catholics disdained Merton because of his stance against the war in Vietnam; because he advocated for interfaith discourse and religious tolerance; and because he protested racial segregation and socio-economic repression of other races, namely African Americans. They reviled Merton because he fought for the Civil Rights Movement with his friends Martin Luther King, Jr., and Rabbi Abraham Heschel, and because during the Cold War he protested the nuclear arms race between America and Russia— a race that could incinerate the world over a small misperception or provocation. Hadn't the Cuban Missile Crisis proved the precariousness of humanity's existence? Many Catholics despised Thomas Merton for eschewing violence and oppression and selfishness, for his disdain of the false marriage of Christianity and capitalism, for the way he loved every person as a brother or sister regardless of color, for having been a peacemaker, for his opposition to antiquated notions of revenge and retribution that disproportionately fills American prisons with people of color, and for his horror at the way so many Christians embrace the death penalty, in spite Christ's message of mercy and forgiveness. It seems to me that some Catholics reviled Merton for wanting to make a heaven on earth, as Jesus spoke of repeatedly.

More than anything else, at the heart of the matter seemed to be the issue of Merton's interest in interfaith discourse. It concerned many American Catholics, especially bishops, that Merton had become so interested in Buddhism. They were terrified that young Catholics might follow in Merton's footsteps and all become Buddhists. Their worry was for nothing. The bishops were all but blind to the truth—that learning about other religions deepened Merton's own Christian faith. In fact, after his three lengthy meetings with the Dalai Lama in Dharmsala, India in November of 1968, the Dalai Lama said, "Thomas Merton introduced me to the real meaning of the word *Christian*." Years later, when asked which three people most influ-

The Naysayers

enced his life, the Dalai Lama named Thomas Merton along with his personal Dharma teacher. It was precisely because of Merton's deep spiritual foundations in his own faith that he could have genuine and respectful dialogue with people from other religious traditions.

Prior to our phone call, I imagined that Fr. Leo's appointment as Interreligious Specialist would have meant that he admired Thomas Merton for the way he reached out to people from other faiths. I would be disingenuous if I told you that Fr. Leo's words did not affect me. They did. They made me sad. They made me question my devotion to a faith that would denigrate such a man while elevating corrupt political leaders who lie about being Christian in order to garner votes from the ignorant, who cheat and lie thousands of times a year; who demean, bully, and abuse women, the disabled, people of other races, and who espouse violence against others. Evangelical and Conservative Christians across the nation—including Catholics—adored a megalomaniac and greedy politician who stated publicly during the 2016 campaign, "When I see money, I want it all," while gesturing as if he were scooping up piles of cash. Those lost Christians forget Jesus's admonishment that you cannot serve both God and money (Matthew 6:24). When asked which biblical attribute most summed up his nature, the greedy politician replied, "Vengeance." They forget Jesus's central teachings about love and compassion and mercy and forgiveness.

Thomas Merton spent the later years of his life fighting for social justice, equality, non-violence, peace, religious tolerance, and even environmental stewardship. He was a supporter of Rachel Carson and her landmark book *Silent Spring* at a time when many opposed it. In fact, he wrote to her. Merton's *The Seven Storey Mountain* is considered one of the quintessential classics of coming-to-faith memoirs, selling millions of copies in many languages. It is often compared to

St. Augustine's *Confessions*.

As a monk following the Rule of St. Benedict, Trappist monks such as Merton took three vows: Obedience, Stability, and Conversion of Manners. The last signifies that monks turn their lives around to follow Christ, and as such, would include a life of poverty and chastity, though they are not explicitly mentioned in the vow. For almost three decades, Thomas Merton lived in a cloistered monastery where he honored his vows and where austerity was the rule. He lived the life of a devoted Christian. He walked the walk and talked the talk.

Fr. Leo wasn't the only Catholic clergy who urged me to destroy the collection. Another priest and even a bishop advised me to destroy everything. One even volunteered to come over to my house and help me do it. He offered to bring a can of gasoline if I didn't have one. I spent many hours in prayer trying to understand why these Catholics despised Merton so much that they would instruct me to destroy his possessions—artifacts that some might even call *relics*—prudently safeguarded by a former monk and nun for half a century. To my way of thinking—as well as that of the former nun—the artifacts deserved to be preserved in museums.

In the end, I am happy to say I did not heed their advice. Yet I wanted to know why some Catholics felt the way they did about Merton. I was bent on learning why Catholic priests would harbor such resentment for a brother priest. I researched the subject assiduously. I read everything Merton published voraciously. I spoke directly to people who knew Merton and who made careers of studying his life and work. I communicated with priests and nuns who knew him personally and who were offended by the way some fellow Catholics have denigrated him over the half century since his death. In the end, I did not destroy a single item in the collection, and the collection has been donated to museums.

What I learned from my ardent studies was that contrary to some specious thinking by conservative American Catholics, Merton was not an outcast or heretic. Indeed, Pope John XXIII and Pope Paul VI both considered Merton to be one of the greatest living Christian writers—especially Paul VI who named Merton among his three favorite spiritual writers. Both popes sent Merton lavish gifts to demonstrate their affection. On Palm Sunday 1960, Pope John XXIII arranged to give Merton an ornate stole he had worn embroidered with gold thread, which is displayed at the Thomas Merton Center. Pope John XXIII was inspired by Merton in writing his April 1963 encyclical *Peace on Earth* (*Pacem in Terris*), in which he wrote that the Christian must above all be a peacemaker. He was quoting Jesus's Sermon on the Mount: "Blessed are the peacemakers, for they shall be called children of God" (Matthew 5:9). Pope John Paul II often quoted Merton in his homilies, and Pope Francis said that Merton inspired him as a young priest. In his address to the U. S. Congress on September 24, 2015, Pope Francis praised Thomas Merton and Martin Luther King, Jr. as being among the greatest Americans, alongside Dorothy Day and Abraham Lincoln. Pope Francis said, "Merton was above all a man of prayer, a thinker who challenged the certitudes of his time and opened new horizons for souls and for the Church. He was also a man of dialogue, a promoter of peace between peoples and religions."

What is there to hate in that?

Plenty if you had asked some American Catholics who believed that Merton was abandoning Catholicism and Christianity and becoming a Buddhist. As an example of the way in which American Catholics have tried to marginalize Thomas Merton, consider how in the early 2000's, U. S. Bishops were working on a young people's catechism which was to include examples of key Catholic figures. At first, Merton was to be included among them, but his name was removed in the final draft by Bishop Wuerl, whom I met during one of my stays at the U. S. Conference of Catholic Bishops Staff House. (By the time I met him, he was a Cardinal.) I recall being introduced to him in a common living room where priests sat around watching television, reading newspapers, or sipping libations from the well-stocked bar. Wuerl had removed Merton's name from the list because of Merton's interest in Buddhism. I wonder what the good Cardinal thought when, in 2015, he sat in the audience as Pope Francis delivered his address to the U. S. Congress in which he extolled Thomas Merton as one of the four greatest Americans.

The more I learned about how some Catholic leaders have tried to suppress, even eradicate, Thomas Merton's memory from history, the more my faith has been shaken to the breaking point.

Let me say that there is absolutely nothing wrong with wanting to learn about other religions, with wanting to learn how other people in other cultures around the world comprehend and worship God, with wanting to learn about other religions' similarities and dissimilarities to our own. In my own life, I count myself fortunate to have observed, even participated in, many religions, from Catholic to Southern Baptist to Unitarian Universalist, from Hindu to Tibetan Buddhist, from traditional Native American religious ceremonies to Passover—as a guest seated beside the rabbi and his family at a synagogue in Brooklyn. I attended one of Rabbi Michael Lerner's last Jewish Shabbat services at Beyt Tikkun. His Torah Study was on the Golden Calf and how and why it angered God and Moses. As a cultural anthropologist fascinated by the influence and perils of religion in society, I took courses in the anthropology and sociology of religion. I studied world religions at Harvard. I took courses in Judaism, Islam, Sufism, and Buddhism, and even studied the historical Jesus.

The Naysayers

As an enrolled member of a tribe in Alaska, I grew up exposed to traditional indigenous beliefs and mythologies as well as Russian Orthodoxy, which is still prevalent in parts of Alaska.

Does any of that make me any less Catholic?

As for Merton, he was interested in monasticism, mysticism, and asceticism as are Buddhist monks and as were the early Christians living in small, secluded and austere communities in the desert. *The Dead Sea Scrolls* came from such a community. Like those hardy desert fathers and St. Augustine centuries before him, Merton wanted to learn more about the efficacy of prayer through concerted meditation, contemplation, and even fasting. It is written that one can only hear God's small voice in silence and stillness. Merton wanted to learn how to hear that small voice more clearly. Silence and stillness are the realms of meditation and mindfulness, not of spectacle and ritual and perfunctory obligations.

Thomas Merton wanted to be a better Christian and to have a richer and deeper spiritual life. He wanted to take what he learned and share it with others so that they too could find their way to a deeper spiritual life. He understood that Christians should not be enraptured by capitalism and materialism—what has come to be called "The Gospel of Prosperity." Echoing St. Ignatius of Loyola, who wrote that followers of Jesus should not prefer riches to poverty, Merton would have said it is absurd and contrary to believe that being rich implies God's favor. Merton was also weary of the inconvenient marriage of Christianity and war-mongering with its incessant mantra of "Might makes right." He loathed bigotry, and the bullying imposition of one group's fanatical beliefs upon everyone else. He had no interest in power or social status. When asked if he would be the next Abbot of Gethsemani, Merton vehemently opposed the idea. In fact, he wrote a letter to the other monks beseeching them not to cast their votes for him. He was content to live his simple existence wearing his simple clothes in his simple cabin in the woods, praying and reading and writing and going on long walks and watching deer, wild turkeys, and woodpeckers from his porch. From those who knew him at the end, Merton's "Christian-ness" was resolute; he was not abandoning Christianity for Buddhism as was rumored by those who saw him as too liberal. If anything, Thomas Merton was increasingly becoming more like Jesus.

And that bothered some Catholics.

Regarding the question of his interest in Buddhism, Thomas Merton answered the question one month before he died—in a letter he wrote to friends back home, from Calcutta on November 9, 1968. The last paragraph of the three-page "Asian Letter I" reads: "I wish you all peace and joy in the Lord and increase of faith: for in my contacts with these new [Buddhist] friends I also feel consolation in my own faith in Christ and His indwelling presence. I hope and believe He may be present in the hearts of all of us." He concludes his letter: "With my very best regards always, cordially yours in the Lord Jesus, and in His Spirit." (signed) Thomas Merton

This hardly sounds like someone who is abandoning his Christian faith.

In many respects, Merton was ahead of his time. He opened the door to what has become commonplace in some religions today, that is, the open and peaceful discourse and exchange among religious practitioners of the world, as Pope Francis proclaimed of the man. Indeed, it was my clergy friends from other denominations—Methodist, Episcopal, Presbyterian, Jewish, United Church of Christ, Unitarian Universalist—all of whom were retired or close to retirement age, who were most excited about my being made guardian of Merton artifacts, and who bolstered my enthusiasm.

To them I am eternally grateful, for they gave me the courage to tell this story.

Fr. Leo's negative opinion of Merton was not unique. It wasn't extreme by any measure. I certainly do not mean to find fault with my friend, only to say that his concerns exemplified the way many Catholics have come to think about Thomas Merton and forced me to dig deeper into the issue, for which I am indebted. Although we disagreed on Merton's repute and on what should be done with his belongings, we remain friends. Eventually, I shared with him what I learned about how previous Popes had admired Merton and considered him to be one of the greatest Christian writers. I shared with him what Pope Francis said about Merton to Congress. Over the years, I even shared several chapters of this book with him and sought his advice on certain topics. Looking back, I think our conversations affected his opinion of Merton, even if only a little. If what I shared was able to change his estimation of Merton, perhaps it can affect the estimations of others as well. Only time will tell.

Since the day the abbot instructed Br. Irenaeus to remove Merton's possessions from the Abbey of Gethsemani, the collection has been assailed by individuals—including Catholic priests—bent on diminishing its contents piece by piece, or destroying it altogether.

It is a miracle it survived at all.

Abbey of Gethsemani or Bust

In the summer of 2015, I contacted the Thomas Merton Center at Bellarmine University in Louisville, Kentucky—the institution where Merton had arranged that his archives should be collected. In a series of emails and phone conversations, I related the history and contents of the trunks to Dr. Paul Pearson, director of the Thomas Merton Center. I recall communicating with the assistant director, Mark Meade as well. I think they were a little skeptical of my story at first. At the same time, Dr. Pearson told me that there was a story he had heard that the abbot back in 1968 had indeed ordered the removal of Merton's possessions, but no one seemed to recall who it was he had given the order to, and no one knew what had happened after that or whether or not the artifacts still existed somewhere. But the story I told him about Sister Mary Pius and Brother Irenaeus seemed to jibe with the story he had heard, enough, that is, that he was satisfied that there was something to the account I related to him. It was agreed that I'd visit him at the Merton Center and talk to him further about the artifacts.

On the drizzly morning of July 20, 2015, I loaded up my black and chrome motorcycle and headed to Louisville, Kentucky, a 500 mile ride. Wanting to avoid interstates out of my white-knuckled fear of semis barreling down the highway at 75 mph, my planned route would take as many back roads as possible, increasing the total distance to more like 550 miles. Besides a change of clothes in my saddlebags, I took my digital camera, which was full of images I had taken of the artifacts inside the trunks, as well as of the trunks themselves, which clearly proved the provenance of the collection. Some of the images were of Brother Irenaeus and Sister Mary Pius, taken by Merton at Gethsemani in 1967 and 1968.

By the time I was thirty miles from home, the sky unleashed a deluge of rain. I was drenched. My thick black leather motorcycle jacket—one of the few things I have to remind me of my dead brother—was soaked and no longer kept me warm. I also wore his high school ring on a chain around my neck. Even my wallet and the cash inside were wet. My leather gloves were soaked. My whole body was trembling, and my teeth were chattering. Yet, I still had more than 500 miles to go, and the sky was dark and gray as far as the eye could see. I took a warm-up break in Hannibal, Missouri, Mark Twain's old stomping ground and the setting of *Tom Sawyer* and *Huckleberry Finn*. I stopped at the McDonald's and changed out of my wet clothes. I was trembling so badly that I could hardly walk or hold anything when I walked through the door.

Everyone was looking at me.

I must have looked like a drenched cat.

I ordered a hot cup of coffee and spent the next hour with my shivering hands wrapped around the paper cup to warm them. I dried my leather jacket and gloves as best I could by using the hot air hand dryer in the restroom. I did the same thing with my wal-

Abbey of Gethsemani or Bust

let and cash. By good fortune, the rain clouds passed. Warm and mostly dry, I decided it was time to continue my eastward journey. After drying my bike seat with paper napkins, I crossed the Mississippi River into Illinois a few minutes later. Almost miraculously, the clouds dissolved and the sun came out in front of me. A few miles later, I pulled over to remove my leather jacket and gloves. I dug out my mp3 player and headphones and resumed my cross-country trek toward Louisville, smiling while Helen Reddy belted out "I Am Woman," one of my favorite songs from the 1970s. (Don't ask me why.) I distinctly remember thinking *Life is good.* There really is something liberating about riding a motorcycle toward an uncertain future.

The freedom of the open road and possibilities, I suppose.

The rest of the first day was uneventful, unlike the time I rode my bike from upstate New York to Madison, Wisconsin in the summer of 2010. On the second day out on *that* trip, I was cruising through Cleveland along Lake Erie during morning rush hour traffic, boxed in by semis hurtling along at 60 mph on a five-lane highway. Suddenly, my oil plug vibrated loose and fell out, instantly coating my rear tire in hot motor oil. The slickened ass of my bike swerved back and forth, left to right, like a fish swimming.

I remember thinking, *This is it! This is the moment of my death.*

Surrounded as I was by eighteen-wheelers, I had imagined myself smeared into the pavement by the crush of a hundred tires before the convoy behind me would stop to see what they had run over ... if they stopped at all. I had applied my brakes, which only made the fish-tailing worse. The rear brake was also coated in hot oil. The only thing I could do was to hang on and ride it out. Swimming like a salmon down the highway at 60 mph or faster, I'd somehow managed to keep the bike upright. Don't ask me how. Because the front tire was dry, I was able to steer the bike toward the grass along the edge of the highway. I shot up the embankment, the incline and grass slowing me down, until the bike and I finally dropped to the ground. Neither the bike nor my body suffered any damage. For a while, I just sat there on the grassy knoll thinking how closely I had come to my own demise, remembering the saying, "It's not *if* a biker will drop his bike; it's *when*."

No one ever stopped to ask if I was all right. And as far as I could tell, the traffic never even slowed down. I recall a few rubberneckers gawking at me as they sped by.

After gathering my wits, I had walked into a nearby neighborhood, knocked on the first door, and asked an old retired African American man for a ride to a motorcycle shop where I bought a new oil plug, a few quarts of oil, a couple rolls of paper towels and a couple cans of engine degreaser to clean the rear tire and brakes. When I was on the road again around noon, I stopped at a gas station and called my friend in Wisconsin to tell him what had happened. I told him I was too shaken to continue the journey, which would take me on interstates around Chicago. Instead, I took back roads all the way home. To this day, I double check that the oil plug is on tight before taking a road trip.

Five years later, en route to Louisville, I stopped for the night at a motel an easy hour's drive from Louisville. The next morning, with plenty of time to spare, I had breakfast at a diner about thirty minutes from the north side of the city. But Bellarmine University, where the Thomas Merton Center is located, was on the far south side, which would add an additional twenty or thirty minutes travel. After a leisurely breakfast, I glanced at my watch. *Lots of time. No hurry*, I thought to myself. But when I went up to the cash register to

Abbey of Gethsemani or Bust

pay, I noticed the clock on the wall behind her, which was one hour later than my watch.

"Excuse me," I said to the cashier. "Is that clock correct?"

She looked at the clock and then at her wristwatch.

"Yes," she replied.

I was dumbfounded. I couldn't understand how I could be so off in my timing. But then I realized that I must have driven across a time zone during the night. I didn't have an hour. I was supposed to meet Paul Pearson in five minutes. In a panic, I called Dr. Pearson and told him of my circumstance, apologizing that I hadn't factored in the time zone difference. I worried he might have thought me an idiot. Fortunately, he told me he could still meet me before his lunch break. I have to say, I was relieved when I hung up. I had come so far. It would have been terrible if we were unable to meet because of a screwup.

I'll never forget our meeting.

I liked Paul immediately. He struck me as a genuinely kind and intelligent individual. We sat down in his office and I recounted the story as I had heard it from Helen Marie, also known to Thomas Merton as Sister Mary Pius. I took out my digital camera and showed him photos of Helen, Brother Irenaeus, and of the trunks and their contents. What caught Paul's attention was a photo of one of the denim jackets with a white square tag sewn on the jacket front. On the tag, written in ink, was the number 127, as well as a couple other numbers which had been struck out. Paul grabbed a book off a nearby bookshelf and handed it to me. There on the cover was a photograph of Merton wearing the jacket. We examined the numbers on the tag closely. It was clear that this was the exact same jacket as I had in one of the trunks back home.

(The author and Paul Pearson at the Thomas Merton Center)

I could see that Paul was elated. I told him that most of the articles of clothing had similar tags with the same number written on them. I asked him about the significance. Paul told me how at the monastery monks were issued clothing, and every piece of clothing had a tag with a number that corresponded to the individual who was assigned them. The tags were used to identify clothing, especially for laundering. Monks could throw their dirty laundry in a bag, which was collected weekly to be laundered. The tags helped to ensure that all clothing was returned to the appropriate owner. Paul told me that for twenty-eight years, Merton's assigned laundry number was 127. He led me over to a glass case in the museum section of the Center and pointed to a large metal safety pin with the number 127 inscribed on it.

"That was Merton's laundry pin. He used it to identify and close his laundry sack."

From that moment on, and perhaps for the first time, I believed Helen Marie. Her story was true. Everything she told me was true. Equally important, Paul Pearson must have felt the same way. A year later, I got a tattoo of Merton's laundry tag and number on my right

Abbey of Gethsemani or Bust

leg to remind me of the whole adventure.

I showed Paul images of photographs that had been in the trunks, some Paul had never seen before. The one that struck him the most was a picture of Merton in his white robe and black scapular sitting on a blanket during one of the summer picnics that he used to go on with Helen Marie and Brother Irenaeus. In the photograph—as seen on the cover of this book—a can of Budweiser sits on the picnic blanket in front of Merton. Paul knew that Merton enjoyed a beer now and then; after all, monks practically invented beer; but he had never before seen a photo of him with a beer.

"I recently gave a presentation about Merton and humor," he said. "The title was a play on Merton's famous quote, 'I love beer; therefore I love the world.' I sure could have used this picture."

After talking in his office, Paul showed me around the museum. On display was a large Cistercian Psalter with its metal locking bracket. I recognized it immediately, for I had one just like it back home. I asked Paul about it. He said it was not Merton's personal psalter, but that it was donated by the monastery to be representative of the kind of psalter Merton would have used in his life at Gethsemani.

"I have Merton's personal psalter," I said, as I fumbled through the images on my camera looking for a picture of it. "Here it is. It was in one of the trunks. It looks just like that one. I could give it to you."

It turned out that another photo in Helen Marie's collection caught the director's eye. There was a snapshot taken of Merton's bedroom in his little cinder block hermitage. The photo showed how Merton had arranged the small room. Flush up against his narrow bed was a tall, four-drawer metal filing cabinet that ostensibly held his notes, letters, drafts, and other papers that he wanted to keep organized. Paul Pearson remarked that there were no known photos of that private part of his hermitage. No one knew how Merton's sleeping room had been arranged or appointed. Needless to say, Dr. Pearson was excited about the photo.

I think we both enjoyed the excitement of that first meeting. It must have felt like Christmas to Paul, the thought of so many of Merton's personal belongings coming to light with the promise of so much of the collection being donated to the Center.

Later, I noticed a series of framed photographs hanging in the hallway outside the Center's main door.

"Merton took those photographs," offered Paul. "A friend of his loaned him a 35 mm camera."

One of the photos caught my attention. It was a photograph of a mountain in Alaska. I recognized it immediately. It was a photograph of a mountain in my tribal region. The mountain even figures in the mythology of my tribe. I know because I've included the myth in several of my books on Alaska Native mythology, including in *The Raven and the Totem*, *In the Shadows of Mountains*, and *Trickster*. Some years back, the Alaska Department of Transportation even posted an interpretative sign about the mountain and the myth at almost precisely the vantage point from which Merton's photograph was taken.

"I know this mountain," I told Paul.

And then I related my connection to it.

"There's a myth that long, long ago, a woman with her baby in a papoose on her back was part of a clan that was moving to the coast. Raven, our deity, told them not to look back at where they had come from, but the young mother missed her old home so much that she looked back. Abruptly, she and her baby turned into the odd-shaped mountain. From a certain angle, you can see the hump that looks like her baby on her back."

Paul had never heard the story before. He was glad to hear it.

"I've even climbed to the top and looked out over the Matanuska Glacier on the other side," I continued. "Heck, I even shot a full-curl Dall sheep up there once. My ex-wife almost fell off a cliff on the way back down in the dark. Luckily, I grabbed one of the shoulder straps on her pack and pulled her to safety."

Paul was curious about my tribe. He wanted to know more about it. I told him where it is located, mostly in villages along the Copper River, and that I had been the tribally-elected executive director of our heritage foundation in the mid-to-late 1990s. I asked him how Merton came to take the photograph. Paul related how, at the beginning of Merton's Asian journey, he had spent some time in Alaska.

I was thrilled. Merton hadn't traveled very often in his twenty-eight years as a monk at Gethsemani, and yet, in the last weeks of his life, he had stood on the land of my tribe and marveled at the rugged beauty surrounding him, awed and inspired enough to snap this photograph. More than that, he had stood at the very same place I have stood many times in my life. The connection was somehow spiritual. I felt a kindred connection to the man that I had not felt before.

Pearson went on to tell me how during that Alaska visit, Merton had spent a week or so in Chugiak/Eagle River, then a small bedroom community about a dozen miles north of Anchorage. He was giving some talks during a religious conference of sorts. I was flabbergasted. I had lived there for twelve years, building two homes for my family with my own two hands. Suddenly, I felt like my role in the discovery of Merton's worldly possessions was less coincidence and more providence. I know that sounds presumptuous, but it's how I felt and how I continue to feel.

Another coincidence that struck me was the fact that if I had not moved to that small Midwest town where I lived and sat at the same place every single morning to write and drink coffee, I would never have learned about Helen Marie and her former monk husband who had lived and worked with Thomas Merton for all those years at the monastery. There were other coincidences. In my early childhood, I'd lived in Kentucky just down the road from the monastery. As an adult, I had studied at the University of Cambridge, just as Merton had once done. My college, Gonville and Caius (est. 1348), was adjacent to Clare College (est. 1326) where Merton had studied more than half a century previous. No doubt we had both strolled along the River Cam and punted in the long, narrow boats that students rent by the hour. We both may have walked the path along the Cam to the small neighboring hamlet of Grantchester and imbibed a pint at the Rupert Brooks Pub. No doubt, we hoisted pints in the same pubs in Cambridge, for some of them are very old. Our love of beer was another thing we had in common. I have no doubt that Merton was familiar with Benjamin Franklin's wise words regarding the libation: "Beer is proof that God loves us and wants us to be happy."

More tragically, we both lost our brother in their twenties. My younger brother, James Ernest, died at 23, while Merton's younger brother, John Paul, died at 24.

Before leaving the Thomas Merton Center, Dr. Pearson gave me some sound advice about the collection. He warned me that as word got out about my "discovery" that some people might reach out to me with offers to purchase artifacts from the collection. He said some zealots might go to any length to obtain what they considered to be religious relics. He told me to exercise caution, and he recommended

Abbey of Gethsemani or Bust

I lock my doors and to be wary of prowlers, for lack of a better word.

After my fruitful visit with Paul Pearson, I took off for the Abbey of Gethsemani, located twelve miles south of Bardstown. It was a perfect summer afternoon. I got a little lost at first, but eventually I found the monastery. I spent the next few hours strolling around the grounds and inside the areas that are open to the public. Downstairs from the main chapel, in an area that is used for retreats and workshops, I saw a painted mural depicting the history of Gethsemani. On the mural was a depiction of Thomas Merton sitting at a small table typing on his old typewriter—which I had just touched earlier that day at the Thomas Merton Center. Although signs around the building reminded visitors that the monastery practiced silence, I was bursting with excitement. I turned to a monk who was cleaning the room and jabbered on about how I had recently discovered a bunch of stuff that used to belong to Merton and that I was on a pilgrimage of sorts. He was kind enough to hear me out, but when I finished talking, he gently reminded me that the monastery is a talk-free zone.

I was a little embarrassed.

Afterward, I hiked up the trail to Merton's hermitage, the small cabin in the woods where he lived for the last few years of his life. Helen Marie had kindly drawn me a map of how to get there from the monastery, as it is still somewhat protected from visitors. I left my motorcycle in the parking lot as I stealthily snuck up the trail, hoping that I wouldn't encounter anyone along the way. I imagined how the trees along the trail were the same trees that saw Merton walking by them, most likely practicing something akin to walking meditation. I took comfort in thinking that the sound of the wind rattling through the leaves was the same sound Merton once heard. When I arrived, I was struck by the smallness of the cabin. Sitting on the edge of the porch, I imagined the clickedy-clack of Merton happily typing away on his manual typewriter. As a writer, I envied Merton's quasi-hermit life. I say quasi because, as I understand it, he took most of his meals with the monks back at the abbey, walking back and forth a couple times a day. Besides, he also had to check to see if there was any mail for him and to send out letters. Renowned figure and prolific writer that he was, Merton was always receiving and sending letters, postcards, and manuscripts.

After a spell, I headed back down the trail, making it back to the monastery without encountering another soul along the way.

Abbey of Gethsemani or Bust

Before leaving Gethsemani, I spent a few minutes at Merton's graveside (above photo). I remember thinking about a photograph I had seen of the Dalai Lama standing at Merton's grave some years after his death. I also remembered that Helen Marie had told me she'd prayed to Father Louis for years to send someone to help her figure out what to do with the trunks. I thanked Merton for letting that someone be me. I told him I was undeserving, but that I would do my best and with the utmost integrity. I promised him that I would work diligently with his old nun friend to donate his possessions to the places where he would have wanted them to be safeguarded and preserved for the future. I also told him about the Thomas Merton Center at Bellarmine University and that I thought he'd be pleased with how well it turned it.

Before leaving, I walked up the green knoll to the giant statue of St. Joseph, remembering the story that Helen Marie had told me about how she and Merton had stood beside that very statue and said their farewells shortly before Merton left for his fateful Asian journey. I remember thinking that I was five years old that day and living in Kentucky. I was most likely playing in the dirt with my matchbox cars, making roads with an old spoon.

With the afternoon waning, I climbed on my motorcycle and headed for Loretto, a dozen or so miles away, where young Sister Mary Pius (Helen Marie) used to live and work at the Sisters of Loretto Motherhouse. Halfway, a cloud burst open and poured rain so hard I could hardly see. Drenched to the bone for the second time on my trip, I remember singing "Kentucky Rain," one of my favorite songs by Elvis Presley.

It turns out that the little hamlet of Loretto is also home to Maker's Mark whisky distillery, famous for the way they dip the necks of their bottles in red wax. Kentucky is full of whisky distilleries, but Maker's

Mark has always been one of my favorites. The Sisters of Loretto Motherhouse was on the other side of town.

Once I arrived, I strolled around the grounds of the convent taking plenty of photographs to show Helen Marie after I returned home. As far as I could tell, the Loretto Motherhouse is a place where infirm nuns go to heal and where old nuns go to die. During her years at the convent, Sister Mary Pius had cared for many of the older nuns. Part of the grounds includes a sweeping cemetery for nuns. Before that day, I had never imagined that such a place existed. There was also a small pond on the right side of the drive just before the main complex of buildings. I remembered a photograph Sister Mary Pius took of Brother Irenaeus standing beside the frozen pond when he came to fetch her one wintry day. The framed picture sat on an end table in her living room full of angels.

After visiting the convent, I felt like I could use a shot of whisky. With the sun skirting the treetops, I steered my bike toward Maker's Mark distillery.

The rest of the journey home was uneventful, except for breakfast the next morning. I stopped at the Waffle House in Elizabethtown, south of the abbey. I was sitting at the long counter when a biker walked in and sat beside me. He was a big guy, close to my age. He looked every bit the stereotype of a bad-ass biker. He wore one of those vests full of patches. After he ordered his breakfast we got to talking.

He introduced himself as "The Deacon". He said he was the leader of a local biker gang.

I noticed the patch on the front of his vest that said, "Bikers for Jesus." I thought it a little ironic. Bikers aren't generally known for their benevolence and nonviolence.

He saw my black leather jacket hanging on the back of my chair.

"That your bike out front?" he asked.

I nodded. I had seen him pull up on a Honda Goldwing instead of on a Harley Davidson. I asked him about it.

"I got a Harley back at the house, but the damn thing's always breaking down. I hate to say it, but these rice rockets run forever."

That's what bikers call motorcycles made in Japan: Kawasaki, Yamaha, Suzuki, and Honda. I've always owned a rice rocket myself. The bike parked out front was a Yamaha 650 cc V-Star Classic—a black and chrome, retro-looking cruiser. I found it a little underpowered for cruising interstates. I eventually sold it and bought a Honda Shadow Sabre, a special edition purple and chrome beauty with flames on the fuel tank and a massive 1100 cc engine beating in its metal chest. With almost double the horse-power, I no longer felt like I couldn't keep up on the interstate. At the same time, it's a lot of bike to handle. It's much heavier than I'm used to.

We talked for a while. I told him I was a university professor and that I was doing research and that I would probably write a book about the trip. He said he had started off in junior college and that he wanted to go on to earn a degree in sociology, but that he never did. I forget what he said he did for a living.

I'll never forget when the Deacon pulled out a Glock .45 auto from inside his vest, ejected the magazine, and handed the pistol to me. I looked around at the faces of the customers and the waitresses and cooks on the other side of the counter. I was really uncomfortable, and pretty sure someone was dialing 9-1-1 to report a biker brandishing a gun at a diner. But, to be honest, no one seemed too concerned. I had the feeling the Deacon was a regular here. Always cautious when it comes to guns, I aimed the pistol at the floor and pulled back the slide to make sure there wasn't a bullet in the chamber. I could tell that my breakfast companion was impressed that I knew my way around handguns.

"Not bad for a f#%ing liberal," he said, nodding with approval. "I always carry that on me. Never know when you're going to need it. A few years back, I killed a man with that gun. We got in an argument about something. He shot first, but I dropped him. Cops said it was self-defense, so I got off."

I glanced at the "Bikers for Jesus" patch again, certain that Jesus didn't pack a concealed handgun and shoot people he didn't agree with and then brag about it to strangers at the local Falafel House. I recalled some lines in the Bible where Jesus said, "Whosoever lives by the sword shall perish by the sword," and his admonishment to "Turn the other cheek."

(The author and The Deacon, Waffle House, Elizabethtown, KY)

I handed back the pistol.

"Let me give you some free advice," said the Deacon, as he shoved the loaded clip back into the butt and then stuffed the pistol back into his vest. "Don't ever call yourself a biker around other bikers.

You hear? You ain't no biker. You're a professor. Being a biker's more than some Middle Class Yuppie riding around on weekends pretending to be a bad ass. Being a biker is a lifestyle. Real bikers will kick your ass for saying you're a biker."

Thinking that every biker probably packs a handgun, I thanked him for his advice.

After breakfast, the Deacon asked where I was headed. I was hesitant to tell him the name of the small town I lived in, back in northeast Missouri, so I simply told him I was going west, toward St. Louis. It was a gorgeous Saturday morning. He asked if he could ride with me for a while. I agreed. For the next hundred miles or so, we cruised down the highway together—me with my cell phone tucked inside my jacket; the Deacon with his Glock .45 auto tucked inside his.

Easy Come, Easy Go

It turned out Paul Pearson was correct to caution me about zealots who might try to purchase, or otherwise acquire, objects from the Merton collection. He said that some folks might not take "no" for an answer. I remember one individual who declared his love and admiration for Merton. He pleaded with me to cut pieces of fabric from Merton's religious garments so he could carry them in a locket. I told him that if I cut pieces of fabric from Merton's clothes for everyone who asked, there would eventually be nothing left of the artifacts to donate to museums for the rest of world. Another individual said he was a collector of Mertonalia, and he asked if he could come visit me in my home with the notion of purchasing specific objects from the collection, or the collection as a whole. He said he had cash. He was insistent on learning my physical address, which concerned me.

Paul Pearson's previous advice came to my mind.

In fact, I related the unsolicited requests to Dr. Pearson. In my paranoia, I found myself double-checking door locks at night, especially the one to the basement where the two trunks from Gethsemani were visible through the windows. I installed one of those battery-operated alarms that alerts if the door is opened even an inch. Much to my wife's chagrin, I also booby-trapped the basement door, as well as an intermediate door, stacking empty tin cans in front of them so that they'd fall over and make a terrible racket should anyone open either door. (In my defense, I was concerned the battery in the electronic alarm might fail.) Many a time, I heard the loud clatter of cans downstairs followed by my wife yelling up to me, "I hate these stupid cans!"

In the end, I am proud to say that I did not concede to any requests to diminish or otherwise break up the collection.

In August, a few weeks after my motorcycle journey to Louisville, Paul Pearson travelled to my house to take possession of the Merton materials. We wasted little time in small talk. He had driven over 500 miles to see the collection. Deep down inside, I think Dr. Pearson worried that his journey might be for nothing, a snipe hunt. He was keen to see the collection. Straightaway, I led him downstairs to the trunks. Both bore labels with the names of the men who shipped them and the address of the abbey, which was different than what it was nowadays. The ship-to labels read simply: "Abbey, Trappist, KY USA." Dr. Pearson explained that the labels on the trunks were in order for the time period and that he recognized the names of the owners. The civilian name on one trunk was Rev. T. Waddell. His monastic name would be Fr. Chrysogonus. I later learned he was a musicologist and composer who once met with Thomas Merton and Joan Baez during her visit to the Abbey (see *Follow the Ecstasy*, p. 129). The other trunk was labelled as having been sent by Rev. C. Peterson.

With a sigh of relief I opened the lids.

Dr. Pearson knelt on the concrete floor and pulled out the first item. I had strategically placed Merton's iconic blue denim jacket with the "127" laundry tag on top. After all, more than any other artifact, it was the one thing that most validated the contents of the collection when I showed the picture of it to Pearson back at Bellarmine University. As Paul lifted up the jacket to behold it in its entirety, I saw tears running down his cheeks. At the time, I supposed they were tears of love for Merton. But Pearson later corrected me in an email, telling me that "it was more complicated than that. I think I was overcome by emotion on seeing and holding such an iconic piece of clothing by a man who had had such a profound impact on my own life—both personally, but also the spiritual and intellectual journey he'd accompanied me on, but also the physical journey, like Merton himself [who had been studying at Cambridge University in England], across the ocean to Kentucky."

No matter the reason, I was profoundly moved by Pearson's emotion. My own eyes welled up to the point I had to look away. But I wept for a very different reason. Mine were tears of absolution for all my doubts. They were tears of affirmation that I had done the right thing by not burning the collection as the influential naysayers had urged me to do.

(Paul Pearson holding Merton's iconic denim jacket and the author. Photo by Amber Johnson; used with permission)

On seeing Paul Pearson's reaction to the artifacts, I knew that others who admired Merton the way he did might have similar responses as they beheld the artifacts close at hand behind glass in some museum. Isn't that why museums exist, to help us connect to the past, both cerebrally and emotionally? The great figures of the past become more real to us—more human—when we witness objects connected to their lives. Imagine viewing Abraham Lincoln's black tall hat from only a foot away in a museum or Benjamin Franklin's iconic rectangular spectacles or the handmade kite he flew during his experiments on electricity. You can almost touch history. It becomes more than simply words on the page of some dry textbook or spouted by some tired and over-worked high school teacher who should have retired years ago. I imagine it's the same reason people go on pilgrimage—to experience their faith more fully.

After going through both trunks, we went upstairs to the dining table to look over a trove of letters, notes, notebooks, and photographs Helen Marie had given me, including a brief letter of recommendation Merton had written to help the former nun get a civilian job. Some of the photographs had never before been seen. One was of Merton sitting on a blanket at a picnic on the monastery's grounds with a can of Budweiser. Another was a group photo of every monk at Gethsemani taken after a new abbot (Flavian) was elected. On the back was a corresponding list of the names of every monk featured, including, of course, Brother Irenaeus and Father Louis.

That evening we enjoyed a marvelous dinner outside on our patio deck. I grilled Alaskan red salmon from the Copper River, the namesake of my tribe. At one point, I telephoned Helen Marie so that Dr. Pearson could thank her personally for her and her late husband's role in safeguarding the collection for so long. I think we were both elated at the outcome of our visit. Dr. Pearson would take back to the Merton Center a priceless treasure of Merton's belongings from his life at Gethsemani, many iconic, and I could rest in the knowledge that the artifacts would be preserved and exhibited publicly for the future. I was content to know that I had fulfilled my promise to the little former nun.

Dr. Pearson stayed the night in our guest room.

The next morning, he wrote in our guest book: "The circle of Merton's friends never ceases to astound me, and you have been key to a remarkable part of that story." After breakfast, I helped Dr. Pearson load up the two trunks in his car. Before setting off, he thanked me for all that I had done to get the collection to him intact. He thanked me for visiting him in Louisville to tell him the story of the monk and the nun and of their friend Thomas Merton. He was glad I had showed him photographs of the collection.

I remember the feeling I had as he drove away. It is rare in the tides of humanity that a single individual has a seat at the table of history. It's difficult to describe, but I felt many different and even conflicting emotions: relief, satisfaction, a sense of pride, but mostly I felt sad that my small role in Thomas Merton's story seemed to be at an end.

I could not have known then that it was not the end.

Franz Jägerstätter: Merton's Model of Moral Courage

Throughout 1967 and 1968, Thomas Merton was working on *Faith & Violence*, a book that would be published around the same time that he left on his fateful Asian Journey in October of 1968. It would be his last book published during his lifetime. We know from letters written in September that Merton received his author's copies from the publisher just before he left. For instance, he sent copies to his friends Ping Ferry and Philip Berrigan. I imagine he also sent a copy to Philip's brother and fellow priest and activist, Daniel Berrigan. I had the good fortune to meet Dan at Fordham University in New York City years ago to talk about my novel-in-progress, *The Gospel of Simon*, which I had been working on for years. I was living in upstate New York at the time, completing a Ph.D. in literature and creative writing at Binghamton University, just down the road from Syracuse where Phil and Dan were raised, and close to Ithaca, where Merton's younger brother, John Paul, had attended Cornell University. In the years before becoming a monk, Merton sometimes traveled to Ithaca to visit his brother (Merton took the train or a bus. He never learned to drive. There's a humorous anecdote about how he once tried to learn to drive one of the monastery's jeeps, but still managed somehow to crash it in an open field). For his lifetime of social justice and peace activism, Dan won the Thomas Merton Prize from the Thomas Merton Center in Pittsburgh in 1988. He passed away in April of 2016, shortly after he received the galleys of my novel.

Like most writers, Merton relished the chance to talk about his own in-progress writing projects. I've never met a writer who didn't, given the opportunity.

Such was the case with *Faith & Violence*.

During their Sunday afternoon jaunts around the monastery grounds in the old jeep, and during their idyllic picnics, Fr. Louis enthusiastically told Sister Mary Pius and Br. Irenaeus about what he was working on. He was particularly keen to tell them about Franz Jägerstätter, an Austrian peasant farmer who, as a young man during World War II, became an increasingly devout Catholic who earnestly studied the Lives of the Saints and who, as a conscientious objector, unfalteringly refused to kill others in the name of Hitler. On March 23, 1933, Hitler gave a speech at the Reichstag in which he stated that the National Socialist "Nazi" Party was founded on Christian principles. He called the Third Reich a Christian Nation. But Jägerstätter was not convinced that Christ would condone Germany's brutal policies of oppression, persecution, and the deliberate execution of German citizens deemed to be unfit to participate in Hitler's ideal state. Christ taught that his followers were to give special care to the most vulnerable among us, not to exterminate them. To the very end, Jägerstätter stood by his conviction that despite Hitler's public assertions, Jesus advocated for nonviolence, not for war.

Franz Jägerstätter: Merton's Model of Moral Courage

The monk and the nun listened intently as Merton described the remarkable life and death of Jägerstätter, while he sat on a picnic blanket and drank a Budweiser.

(Fr. Louis talking about Franz Jägerstätter during a picnic, c. May 1968; Photo by Helen Marie; used with permission)

Merton had learned about Jägerstätter from his American sociologist friend and fellow peace movement activist, Gordon Zahn, who, in 1964, published *In Solitary Witness: The Life and Death of Franz Jägerstätter*. Zahn had learned about Jägerstätter while researching for a book in 1956. The book brought international attention to the almost forgotten story of Franz Jägerstätter's nonviolent protest against Hitler's Nazi war machine. Motivated by Zahn and utterly convinced that more Catholics needed to hear the story, Merton included an entire chapter about Jägerstätter in *Faith & Violence* (1968).

In a coincidence too great to ignore, at the time I met former Sister Mary Pius and was entrusted with the trunks full of Merton's worldly possessions, I was working on a young adult novel set in Germany during the last months of WWII. *The Field* (*Das Feld*) is the story of a teenage German boy named Wilhelm, whose character is based loosely on Franz Jägerstätter. Willy's father was a professor of religion and philosophy at a university before he was fired for failing to embrace the Nazi Party. Like Franz Jägerstätter, Willy also wrestles with his conscience. In my research, I reached out to Jägerstätter's only living daughter, Maria Dammer-Jägerstätter, who was still living in Austria. Maria was almost eighty years old. With some help from the Friends of Franz Jägerstätter Society in upstate New York, Maria and I exchanged a series of emails through a friend of hers, who spoke English. She was glad I was writing my book, and she kindly provided an afterword to accompany it, for which I am eternally grateful.

(The author in Vienna, fall 2015.
Photo by Amber Johnson; used with permission)

Franz Jägerstätter: Merton's Model of Moral Courage

In the fall of 2015, I spoke at an international anthropological conference on hunter-gatherers at the University of Vienna. My talk was on contemporary Alaska Native subsistence issues. I tried to set up a face to face meeting with Maria, but sadly, her health was failing, and she was unable to meet me. Instead of me telling you about her father, I thought it prudent to let her tell you about her courageous father in her own words:

(Franz Jägerstätter, c. 1940)

My father, Franz Jägerstätter, was an Austrian peasant with a strong moral conscience. In 1940, he was conscripted to serve in the German Army and completed basic training. In February of 1943, he was called to active duty and given a choice: take the Nazi military oath to fight and kill for the Third Reich, or be killed himself. My father stood by his conviction as a conscientious objector and refused to harm others in what he saw as Hitler's unjust and unprovoked war. His decision was not out of fear or cowardice, but out of courage and conscience. From prison he wrote: "I cannot and may not take an oath in favor of a government that is fighting an unjust war.... I cannot turn the responsibility for my actions over to the Führer. Does anyone really think this massive bloodletting can bring Europe to a new flowering? Is it more virtuous to offer oneself as a victim right away rather than first have to murder others just to prolong one's own life a little while longer?"

Many people tried to persuade my father to change his mind, including the Bishop of Linz, who encouraged him to fight and kill and die for the Reich, saying, "How can the government be wrong? The Führer knows best." Imagine that ... priests and bishops condoning the wholesale murder of millions of people.

(Private Franz Jägerstätter, c. 1940. Photo used with permission of Maria Dammer-Jägerstätter)

But my father would not be intimidated into conformity. And so, on August 9, 1943, after half a year in prison, the

Gestapo executed him by guillotine for his uncompromising beliefs. I was a little girl at the time. My father gave up his life rather than take the lives of other people who had done him no harm. In doing so, he resisted the evil, tyrannical, anti-human political machinery of Nazi Germany.

In 2007, my father was declared a martyr and beatified in Linz by Pope Benedict XVI, a step toward sainthood. It is important for people—especially for young people—to have such a role model for decisions of conscience and to consider whether something is good and right and just, or simply to go along with the fanaticism and hysteria of the mob.

(Maria Jägerstätter [middle] c. 1939. Photo used with permission of Maria Dammer-Jägerstätter)

In her poignant afterword, Maria Dammer Jägerstätter recounts how the Bishop of Linz visited her father in prison several times in an attempt to convince him to declare his allegiance to Hitler and to go fight and kill in Hitler's name. He tried to convince her father that it was morally permissible for a Christian to save himself by assenting to kill others as one's duty to country. But Jägerstätter saw through the fallacy of the Bishop's argument. In every way, Germany was the aggressor. No foreign government had attacked Germany. There was no defending the Fatherland. What honor or duty was there in participating in a campaign of terror? Jägerstätter saw the war for what it was: a monstrous attempt to conquer the world and rid it of millions of undesirable human beings and to steal their lands. From his calculated rhetoric, his wholesale assault on race, his cult-like hold on his followers and from his insidious and relentless propaganda about patriotism and his references to making Germany great again, Hitler turned Germany into a den of murderers and thieves. He called any newspaper or radio station that dared question his actions and policies "Unpatriotic" and "Enemies of the People."

Jägerstätter was undeterred by the bishop's unsuccessful pleas. Time and again he quoted the Gospels, citing lines straight from the mouth of Jesus. "But how can we be followers of Jesus and embrace the wholesale murder of millions at the same time?" he asked. The Bishop grew frustrated at Jägerstätter's steadfast refusal to murder for the State, even at the cost of his own life. His Christian resolve made the Bishop look bad. The Bishop began to feel ashamed. Here was a poor and uneducated farmer showing him what it truly means to be Christian. Exasperated, the Bishop threw up his hands and shouted, "I'm a Bishop! You're nothing compared to me! How is it I am loyal to Hitler while you are not? Do you think you are better than me?"

Though he never said it (I will say it for him), Jägerstätter was a better Christian than His Eminence, the Bishop.

Sadly, it is an historical fact that some priests and bishops within the Reich aligned with the Nazis, especially after Hitler's proclamation in 1933 that the Party was founded on Christian principles—glad news to a citizenry that considered Germany a Christian Nation. There is no shortage of photographs showing Catholic clergy posing in the Nazi salute beside German officers. But this point should be made clear: Contrary to popular belief since the 1960s, the Roman Catholic Church as an institution did not condone the Nazi's genocidal pogrom against the Jews. The fallacy arises from Rolf Hochhuth's controversial and popular 1963 play, *The Deputy: a Christian Tragedy*, which intentionally distorted historical facts. Coincidentally, Merton wrote a critique of *The Deputy*, which is included in *The Literary Essays of Thomas Merton* (162-167). In reality, Pope Pius XII may have feared that if he denounced the Nazi atrocities too strongly, Hitler would order the occupation and dismantling of the Church as a threat against the Third Reich (as he had done in parts of Eastern Europe). In public, Pope Pius XII upheld a policy of neutrality, lobbied for peace and support for war victims, while at the same time waging a clandestine resistance against the Nazis, even giving refuge to thousands of Jews secreted inside Vatican-controlled religious houses in Rome.

A number of films have recently been made about Jägerstätter and about the Vatican's stance regarding the Third Reich's aggressions in Europe during WWII, including the Holocaust. Some of these include: *Franz Jägerstätter: A Man of Conscience* (2011), *A Hidden Life* (2019), and *A Hand of Peace* (2009).

Around the same time that Zahn and Merton were working on their respective books, Pope John XXIII convened the Second Vatican Council (commonly referred to as Vatican II), which lasted from 1962-1965. The Council's objective arose from a desire for reform, reconciliation, and inter-religious tolerance in the aftermath of WWII. Decades later, in April of 2016, eighty-five prominent Catholic peacemakers from around the world participated in a three-day conference at the Vatican to encourage the Church to expand on Vatican II and declare that there is no such thing as a "just war," and that in keeping with the gospels, the Church cannot condone the killing of human beings under any circumstances. In the end, the participants called on Pope Francis to write an encyclical to reject just war theory once and for all. In an action that Franz Jägerstätter would have applauded, the Vatican released the following statement: "Jesus was nonviolent; that there is no just war; that nonviolence works; and that the time has come for the [Catholic] Church to apply and teach nonviolence around the world."[2]

Helen Marie told me that in a number of conversations between her and Merton in 1968, especially after the assassinations of Martin Luther King, Jägerstätter's example of moral courage clearly had a profound effect on Merton, who began to feel that his actions of protest against the unjust war of aggression in Vietnam paled in comparison to Jägerstätter's sacrifice (he said as much in his "Fall 1968 Farewell Letter to Friends"). After all, what did he risk? A few hate letters in the mail? Some negative opinions of him published in newspapers calling him an unpatriotic liberal? (In an interview, Helen Marie told me that Thomas Merton was talking about Jägerstätter at the moment the photograph on the cover of this book was taken.)

People like Martin Luther King, Jr. and the thousands of Civil Rights marchers including Rabbi Abraham Heschel risked their safety and freedom in the name of social equality and peace. King lost his life in the pursuit. On April 5, 1968, Merton wrote to King's widow, Coretta, after his assassination, to send his condolences. He wrote: "In imitation of his Master he has laid down his life for his friends and enemies.... He will go down in history as one of our greatest citizens." The first line, a reference to John 15:13, was much on Merton's mind throughout 1968. All across the nation people were

---

[2] See Terrance Ryan, "The Pope Has Already Taught Non-Violence: Let's Put it in an Encyclical" *National Catholic Reporter* 2 Dec. 2020 for further discussion.

taking action by marching and staging protests. In some instances, protesters were mercilessly beaten by the police. Take for example the civil rights march across the Edmund Pettus Bridge in Selma on March 7, 1965 when over 500 peaceful marchers were brutally attacked by lawmen armed with billy clubs and tear gas. King and his followers knew that injustice prospers when people of conscience do nothing. The way Merton saw it, all he did was to sit in the safety of his hermitage in the woods writing letters and articles and books.

During their pleasant outings, Merton told Sister Mary Pius and Brother Irenaeus how he felt increasingly ashamed, the way he imagined the Bishop of Linz must have felt deep down inside. Over in Vietnam, the corpses were piling up on both sides, their deaths were for nothing. There was no end to the war in sight. Merton told his two friends that he felt like a coward. He felt impotent. Only a few years earlier, in *Seeds of Destruction* (1964), Merton wrote, "If God has become Man [through Jesus] then no Christian is ever allowed to be indifferent to man's fate. Whosoever believes that Christ is the Word made flesh believes that every man must in some sense be regarded as Christ.... If we are Disciples of Christ, then we are our brother's keepers" (96). Merton needed to do something. He needed to "be his brother's keeper." He needed to be more like Jesus, who went to Jerusalem on that fateful Passover despite the danger that he knew awaited him. Jesus himself said that it was not a man's words that mattered, but his actions.

In the immediate years before his death, Thomas Merton must have ruminated over Jesus's counsel, "Blessed are the peacemakers, for they will be called the children of God" (Matthew 5:9) and "There is no greater love than to lay down one's life for friends" (John 15:13). He wanted to be a peacemaker. He needed to do something that mattered, to risk something in the name of God and Christ and in the name of Love.

But what could he do?

Slowly, a plan took root in his mind. Half a century later—especially after former Brother Irenaeus passed away in 2009—only one living human being knew for certain what his plan was.

The cat was almost let out of the bag during a dinner conversation in January of 2016.

Enacting Love

Helen Marie joined my family on a road trip to Louisville in late January of 2016 to visit the Thomas Merton Center at Bellarmine University and to attend the first exhibit of some of the objects from the Grimes-Smelcer Thomas Merton Collection at the Frazier Museum. My in-laws joined us. Although Paul Pearson had spoken to Helen Marie on the phone when he visited our house the summer before, this visit was the only time Paul Pearson ever met with the former nun.

We visited the Thomas Merton Center earlier in the day. Helen Marie was visibly delighted as Paul showed us around the Center. At times, Helen Marie was tickled with excitement. At other times, her eyes were tear-filled from the emotions that welled up. She recognized many of the objects on display from his hermitage: Merton's manual typewriter, his 35mm camera (given to him by a friend), and many other items on display. She took great delight in seeing some of the objects from the trunks finally on display.

(Helen Marie and Paul Pearson at the Thomas Merton Center)

She grabbed my arm when she saw the colorful hood that Merton had received when the University of Kentucky bestowed an honorary doctoral degree on Merton in 1967. She leaned close to the glass to read the name of the donor.

"That wasn't his to give," she whispered. "It came from one of my trunks. It wasn't his."

For the rest of the trip and on the long drive home, she kept bringing up the subject of how the doctoral hood had been taken from her in the early 1970s. Over and over, she related the story of how her old boss at the greasy diner had made her give it to him. She wanted me to correct the error.

I told her I'd try.

Later that afternoon, we drove over to the Frazier Museum to attend the opening of an exhibit entitled "A Familiar Stranger: From the Collections of the Thomas Merton Center at Bellarmine University." Patrons were greeted by a giant black and white photo of Merton holding up his camera as if to photograph them while they milled about (see photo below).

Enacting Love

(From left to right: Frazier Museum Director, Penny Peavler, Paul Pearson, Helen Marie, and the author at the Frazier Museum. Photo by Dan Johnson. Used with permission)

At one point in the program, one of the organizers stood up and introduced Helen Marie and told the audience about her friendship with Thomas Merton and how she and her deceased husband—one of Merton's brother monks—had safeguarded Merton's possessions for all these years. After he announced that some of the artifacts seen on display had been hers and that she had recently donated them to the Thomas Merton Center, the audience erupted into an enthusiastic standing ovation. I stepped back to give her room to enjoy the moment all by herself. Even now, I can feel her heart overflowing with pride and love for her old mentor. Even now, I can see her standing beside me smiling with tears of pride and joy running down her cheeks. Even now, I have tears in my eyes just thinking about it.

It was the only time Helen Marie received public recognition for what she had done. Helen Marie and I had a chance to meet the president of Bellarmine University, Dr. Joseph J. McGowan. I remember asking President McGowan to keep supporting the Thomas Merton Center, which is housed at Bellarmine. He promised he would. Sadly,

Dr. McGowan passed away not long after this photo was taken.

(Helen Marie, Bellarmine President McGowan, and the author; Photo by Dan Johnson. Used with permission)

After the opening at the Frazier, Paul Pearson took us all out to dinner at the Bristol Bar & Grill, an upscale restaurant in Louisville. At one end of the long table sat Helen Marie, myself, and Paul Pearson. Mark Meade, the assistant director of the Thomas Merton Center, sat at the other end of the table with his family and my wife and our daughter, who was five years old at the time. My in-laws sat in the middle. At one point during the conversation, Paul Pearson, Helen Marie, and I began talking about Merton's death. Pearson quietly mentioned to me and Helen Marie that he believed Merton might have been killed by the C.I.A. because he had planned to sneak into North Vietnam and surrender himself to the North Vietnamese as a "hostage for peace"—in order to influence public sentiment against the war and possibly to bring about its early end, thereby saving countless lives.

Enacting Love

(Helen Marie and Paul Pearson at the Bristol Bar & Grill)

I remember that, on hearing Pearson's remark, Helen Marie and I exchanged knowing glances, for she had already told me that Thomas Merton had planned to do precisely that. I surreptitiously put a finger to my lips, signaling to her not to say anything. I didn't think the setting was the right occasion to disclose what we knew. As Helen Marie had once told me, it was not yet the "acceptable time." I had to hold my tongue and use my poker face, which isn't very convincing. It was a hard secret to keep. It would be a few years before I told Paul Pearson what Merton had said to Helen Marie in the days before he left on his fateful journey.

I was struck by the term "hostage for peace." Helen Marie always said "peace prisoner" when she spoke of Merton's plan. Years later, Pearson clarified what he'd meant that evening, saying that according to Merton's friend, Jim Forest, it was Daniel Berrigan—the Jesuit priest, social activist, and anti-war protester—who had suggested to Merton the idea of a going to North Vietnam as a "hostage for peace," or as a human shield. I later learned that Merton had written about the conversation on May 10, 1967, in what have come to be called his *restricted journals*, attesting that he and Daniel Berrigan did indeed discuss the idea. (See chapter, "Pieces of a Puzzle.") Although I had met with Fr. Berrigan at Fordham University in 2006, during his time as Fordham's Poet-in-Residence, I had not yet heard about the trunks full of Merton's belongings until almost a decade later, so our conversation never turned in that direction. In retrospect, I wish I had asked him whether or not he had suggested the idea to Merton. But from what I know of Berrigan and his unconventional methods of activism and protest, it certainly sounds like something he or his brother, Philip, would have proposed.

It turns out that The Bristol Bar & Grill is literally across the street from where Helen Marie and Robert used to live at 1620 NE Rosewood after getting married in December of 1969, and where for fifteen years the trunks full of Merton's worldly possessions were safely stowed, unbeknownst to almost anyone. Even Abbot Flavian had been unaware that Merton's possessions were still intact, stored in metal trunks in Louisville just fifty miles up the road from the monastery. As far as he knew, the artifacts had been destroyed. Even fifty years later, rumors persisted that the collection had been destroyed, burned on the abbot's orders. After dinner, we did a drive-by, parking along the curb to allow Helen Marie time to reminisce about those early years together as husband and wife. She pointed out the window to the guest bedroom where Sister T. had stayed when she visited them in 1970.

In the spring of 2017, two years after my initial "discovery" of the Merton trunks, Paul Pearson happened upon a letter that substantiated all of the things Helen Marie had said to us about her two years of living near Gethsemani and her close friendship with Thomas Merton. He sent me a copy of the three-page letter written by Br. Benedict (named after the monk whose "Rule" is followed by

Trappists) to John Howard Griffin (Merton's biographer) on August 20, 1971. In the typed letter, Br. Benedict reports what he knew or had heard about "a Mrs. Robert Grimes," a "former contemplative nun." He wrote that she "got in touch with Louie, and he arranged for her to come here for some direction and he got her a job as a lay helper over at the Sisters of Nazareth of Loretto" [sic] where "she lived for two years in this capacity." He wrote how during those two years, Brother Irenaeus would pick her up and bring her to Sunday Masses at Gethsemani. He also mentioned that Merton was her spiritual teacher: "I think, also that Fr. Louis gave her direction, now and then. Her name is Helen Marie." (He had originally typed her name as Helen Louise or Helen Therese, but he struck out both names and wrote in blue ink Helen Marie.) Br. Benedict went on to say the monk and nun eventually got married, and he even stated that their marriage was celibate, just as Helen Marie had told me (the entire letter was about "spiritual marriages"). In fact, mirroring what Helen Marie told me about the nature of their marriage, Br. Benedict wrote: "As far as I know, they have lived in this way for the past year and a half with success." (Letter of Br. Benedict, August 20, 1971, p. 2).

I think Dr. Pearson was genuinely glad for Br. Benedict's corroboration of Helen Marie's remarkable story. I know I was. All of the pieces were fitting together. As I have said previously, I have never had any reason to doubt the things she told me. Through five decades, Helen Marie quietly safeguarded her beloved mentor's belongings without fanfare, never reaching out to tell her story to any journalist. Clearly, she was not seeking fame or public accolades.

A Distillation of Faith

Even if Daniel or Philip Berrigan, or someone else had suggested to Merton the idea that he surrender himself as a "peace prisoner" or "hostage for peace" to the North Vietnamese while he was in Southeast Asia, would Merton have seriously considered the notion? If the kinds of things Merton was studying at the time are any indication of the evolution of his thinking on war and peace and justice, then the answer is a resounding *yes*.

In *Seeds of Destruction* (1964) Thomas Merton was forming his conviction that, above all else, a Christian must be a peacemaker. He was internalizing Jesus's instruction from his Sermon on the Mount: "Blessed are the peacemakers, for they shall be called children of God" (Matthew 5:9). From reading works like *Contra Celsum* by Origen (c. 185 - c. 254 C.E.), also known as Origin of Alexandria or Origin Adamantius—an important early Christian scholar, ascetic, and theologian who helped to lay the foundations of philosophical theology for the church—Merton learned that it is not only right but obligatory to disobey human laws when they are contrary to the law of God: "We no longer take the sword against any nations nor do we learn war any more since we have become the sons of peace through Jesus," he wrote (*Seeds*, 139). Other early Christian apologists like

Clement of Alexandria (150 – 215 C.E.), a contemporary of Origen, reminded Followers of Jesus that Jesus was the "Prince of Peace," and condemned military service altogether. Justin Martyr (100 – 165 C.E.) declared that the Followers of Jesus "do not make war upon our enemies." Merton often referred to the writings of Tertullian (155 – 240 C.E.), who declared that when "Jesus took away Peter's sword in the Garden of Gethsemani he disarmed every soldier thereafter who would call themselves his followers" (*Seeds*, 134).

From Origen and Clement and other early Christian theologians, Merton was learning that "the Christian does not help the war effort of one particular nation, but he fights against war itself with spiritual weapons. Love . . . must underlie all Christian action (141)." *Action* was beginning to take on more meaning for Merton. You could tell by the tone in his late writing that Merton was disappointed that St. Augustine's thoughts on war took such tenacious root in Christianity, giving permission for Christians to kill for the state, despite God's commandment, "Thou shall not kill." Merton appreciated how St. Cyprian (c. 200 - c. 258 C.E.) observed that when one individual murders another it is abhorrent, but "when homicide is carried out publicly on a large scale by the state it turns into a virtue" (*Ad Donatum*, VI, 10).

More than any other Christian writer, St. Augustine opened the door for what Merton saw as the unholy marriage between Christianity and the State, and especially the military. He was repulsed by the way some Christians considered themselves to be "Soldiers for Christ." Merton suspected that the peculiar bedfellow relationship between American government and religion was not coincidental. Like some Machiavellian scheming to maintain power at any price, the relationship was purposefully nurtured by the state, which wanted to use religion for its own purposes, despite the fact that the framers of

A Distillation of Faith

the U.S. Constitution knew that the powers of religion and state must be separated because of the inherent dangers evidenced by history. Journals and letters by the Founding Fathers clearly indicate that America was not founded on any notions of religion. It was founded on Roman and Greek principles of democracy. Some of the language of our Constitution comes directly from those ancient writers and philosophers.

On reading the writings of those early Church fathers who lived at a time much closer to when a living Jesus walked the earth, Merton understood that "the state tends to usurp the powers of God and to blaspheme Him, setting itself up in His stead as an idol, and drawing to itself the adoration and worship that are due to God alone" (*Apocalypse* 13:3-9, from *Seeds*, 130). He recognized how the leader of the state is grossly revered as a messiah who has come as a savior like Jesus—only without any of the redeeming, moral qualities of Jesus such as humility, compassion, mercy, honesty, forgiveness, inclusion, and nonviolence. Certainly, history bears this out. One has only to consider Hitler and how he cunningly distorted and transformed the Nazi Party into a quasi-religious institution, an idol demanding allegiance and adoration by its subjects. Akin to falsehearted politicians today, Hitler gave a speech to the Reichstag on March 23, 1933 in which he described Christianity as the foundation for the National Socialist "Nazi" Party. For the despot who understands that power is an end of itself, usurping the power of religion is a tool to control the masses. Hitler claimed that he would make Germany great again. "Drain the Swamp!" was one of Mussolini's standards. By the late 1930s, any member of German society who did not embrace the Nazi Party or revere Hitler as a God-figure was labelled as "unpatriotic" and a "traitor." Newspapers or radio stations that published negative stories about him or his policies were called "enemies of the people."

Sound familiar?

In reading early Church figures like Origen, Clement, Cyprian, Ignatius, Polycarp, Tertullian, Hippolytus, Eusebius, Gregory of Nyssa, Justin, and Irenaeus, Bishop of Lyons (Brother Irenaeus' namesake), Merton also came to appreciate the role of martyrdom in early Christianity. In *De Anima*, Tertullian wrote that "you must take your cross and bear it after your Master.... The sole key to unlock Paradise is your own life's blood" (55; from Pagels, 88). On martyrdom (*martyrium*), Irenaeus wrote: "The Church alone sustains with purity the reproach of those who suffer persecution for righteousness' sake, and endure all sorts of punishments, and are put to death because of the love which they bear toward God, and their confession of his Son" (AH 4:33:9, from Pagels, 89).

In addition to the writings of those early church fathers, Merton also studied the works of Meister Eckhart (c. 1260 - 1328 C.E.), the German theologian, philosopher, and mystic from whom he learned the central tenet of compassion: "What happens to another, be it be a joy or a sorrow, happens to me." Merton wrote often that Eckhart was his spiritual lifeboat. At the same time, Merton was reading the work of more contemporary writers like Dietrich Bonhoeffer (1906 -1945), the German Lutheran pastor, theologian, and anti-Nazi dissident who was arrested by the Gestapo in April of 1943, two years after Merton's arrival at the doorstep of the Abbey of Our Lady of Gethsemani, where the abbot asked him the question that is asked of every man who comes with the desire to be a monk and to live among the austere brethren: *Quid petis*? What do you ask (i.e. Why do you come here?). Merton may have taken the title of his book, *Seeds of Destruction*, from Bonhoeffer's *Letters & Papers from Prison* (p.8). In fact, from his handwritten notes, we know that Merton read *Letters & Papers* in the summer of 1964. No doubt, Bonhoeffer, like Jägerstätter, was on Merton's mind in 1968. Bonhoeffer was a staunch critic of Hitler's euthanasia program and his genocidal persecution of the Jews. He was accused of taking part in a plot to assassinate Hitler and executed by hanging at Flossenbürg Concentration Camp on April 9, 1945 as the war that Germany had started was coming to an end and as Germany was being bombed mercilessly into oblivion, day and night, its women and girls raped by Russian soldiers eager for revenge for what the German soldiers had done to their wives and mothers and daughters on the Russian Front and elsewhere in Europe during their reign of terror.

So much for any notion that Hitler's new Germany—The Third Reich—was founded on Christian principles as he had once declared to the mob gathered outside the steps of the Reichstag.

By the mid-to-late 1960s, Merton was beginning to understand that America, too, was "usurping the powers of God and ... setting itself up in His stead as an idol, and drawing to itself the adoration and worship that are due to God alone." Franz Jägerstätter understood this about Germany when he wrote from a Nazi prison before he was executed by guillotine: "Is it right and just to kill for Hitler just because he says it is right and just to do so?" Uneducated as he was (though he had studied the *Lives of the Saints*), Jägerstätter had come to understand that the Followers of Jesus do not kill. They abhor violence and war. He understood in his heart of hearts that the Follower of Jesus must, first and foremost, be a peacemaker.

Like Jägerstätter and Bonhoeffer, Merton came to realize that the State—and he was thinking especially of America—had hijacked St. Augustine's writings on the Christian and the just war, abusing Augustine to its own benefit by persuading Christians that it is right to kill and die for the State if the State says so, in direct contrast to God's commandment: "Thou shall not kill" and Jesus's saying that

"He who lives by the sword shall perish by the sword." Merton wept for Christian Americans hoodwinked into believing that our government and Jesus or God were one and the same, or on equal footing. He was learning that America was not the "Christian Nation" it claimed to be.

In one of his many correspondences that have come to be known as the "Cold War Letters," Thomas Merton wrote to Rabbi Everett Gendler in October of 1962, saying that while he supported wholeheartedly the efforts of the peace movement to communicate new ideas against a tidal wave of propaganda, "at the same time I am impressed with the fact that all these things are little more than symbols. Thank God they are at least symbols, and valid ones. But where are we going to turn for some really effective political action? As soon as one gets involved in the machinery of politics one gets involved in its demonic futilities and in the great current that sweeps everything toward no one knows what" (Thomas Merton, Cold War Letter 111, to Rabbi Everett Gendler, Princeton, October 1962; in *Thomas Merton, Witness to Freedom: Letters in Times of Crisis*, edited by William H. Shannon).

Throughout the 1960s, Merton was wrestling with America's collective lack of compassion for other human beings and the way in which we cast aside sanity when it comes to how we regard others. He was frustrated with our reckless and blind obedience to religion as well as to politics. He was concerned that our moral compass was broken—north was south, east was west, and up was down. "What is sanity in the modern world?" he wondered. He was thinking about the way African Americans were treated in America a hundred years after Emancipation. He was thinking about the systemic inequalities between rich and poor—the *Haves and Have Nots*. He was thinking about our unjust wars in East Asia, the wholesale destruction of peo-

A Distillation of Faith

ple who had done nothing to America, but who simply embraced a different form of government. In *Raids on the Unspeakable* (1966), Merton writes:

> "The whole concept of sanity in a society where spiritual values have lost their meaning is itself meaningless.... And so I ask myself: what is the meaning of a concept of sanity that excludes love, considers it irrelevant, and destroys our capacity to love other human beings, to respond to their needs and their sufferings, to recognize them also as persons, to apprehend their pain as one's own? Evidently this is not necessary for sanity at all." (46-47)

If Merton were alive today, he would be appalled by the way media enflames anger and hatred, intolerance and violence by manufacturing mass psychosis and hysteria through the calculated dissemination and sheer repetition of lies. He would wonder if sanity can ever return to an insane world.

In *Seeds of Destruction*, Merton frequently cites Pope John XXIII's 1963 encyclical *Pacem in Terris* (*Peace on Earth*). Thinking especially about American politics, Merton writes that the politician

> should not be a ruthless and clever operator with unlimited power at his disposal, justified in taking any decision that serves him and his party or nation in the power-struggle. He must be—as Pope John says—a "man of great equilibrium and integrity," who is competent and courageous.... And he must not evade his basic moral obligations for "reasons of state." On the contrary, statesmen and governments, which put their own interests before everything else, including justice ... are no better than bandits (165).

Even in the mid-1960s, Merton understood America's increasing, yet mistaken, desire for isolationism and nationalism. In *Seeds of Destruction* (Merton may have borrowed his book title from a line in Bonhoeffer's *Letters & Papers from Prison*), he wrote:

> "We must condemn all isolationism and nationalistic individualism which might prompt a government to seek its own interests, ignoring and holding in contempt the rest of the world. At the present time all of the countries in the world are so closely inter-related that no one nation can simply turn upon itself and seek its own advantage without affecting other nations. No country should unjustly oppress other countries or meddle in their affairs." (166-167)

Albert Einstein, a contemporary of Merton who escaped Hitler's gas chambers, also knew this to be true when he wrote in *In Our Time*: "The greatest obstacle to world peace is that monstrously exaggerated spirit of nationalism, which also goes by the fair-sounding name of patriotism. It seriously threatens the survival of civilization and our very existence. Only by overcoming our national egotism will we be able to contribute towards improving the lot of humanity." (33)

America—indeed the world—would do well to learn from Merton and Einstein.

Thomas Merton realized, finally, that in a world of insanity where so many suffer—often because of injustice and lack of caring, mercy, compassion, and tolerance—that prayer was not enough. Like Meister Eckhart, Dietrich Bonhoeffer, and Jesus before them, Thomas Merton came to understand that *action* is necessary. Bonhoeffer called such liberating acts "responsible action." Buddhists call it "right ac-

A Distillation of Faith

tion." Faith demands actions of love. Love means compassion. And compassion means justice. There is a reason that actions to alleviate the suffering of others are called *good works*. From what he observed from the Civil Rights Movement, Merton would say that change requires more than prayer. He would say that real change requires action. Like the late Congressman John Lewis, who carried *The Seven Storey Mountain* in his backpack as he marched across the Edmund Pettus Bridge on March 7, 1965 into the waiting hands of baton and billy club-wielding police, Thomas Merton appreciated that accomplishing good works meant that feet must meet pavement.

Having studied the simple, yet enduring writings of the early desert fathers—those hardy men in the second through fourth centuries who created some of the earliest ascetic Christian communities in the deserts of Egypt and Palestine—Merton was reminded that above all else, the single most important virtue of a Follower of Jesus is charity, intentional action to relieve the sufferings of others. As he wrote in the introduction of his little pocketbook, *The Wisdom of the Desert* (1960), "The Coptic hermits who left the world as though escaping from a wreck, did not merely intend to save themselves.... They had the obligation to pull the whole world to safety after them" (36). Throughout the writings in the *Verba Seniorum* ("Words of the Elders") is the insistence of the power of love over everything else. For those men, as for Merton, love is the Spiritual Life. Without love, everything else, including religion itself, is empty and illusory. Of Merton's little collection of the sayings of the Desert Fathers, our mutual friend, Dan Berrigan, wrote, "Merton does not so much introduce the Fathers of the desert; he stands in their midst, one of them."

But he did not yet stand among them.

There was work to be done.

By the fall of 1968, Thomas Merton was no longer content to just sit in the solitude and safety of his hermitage in the pastoral hills of Kentucky where he had spent the past three years writing articles and letters and books while risking nothing but the cost of stamps and envelopes while so many others, like his friends Dan and Phil Berrigan, and especially Martin Luther King, Jr., had risked so much. He felt his efforts were increasingly barren and ineffective, even cowardly. He could sit no longer. He felt like he needed to go out and "pull the world to safety," to wrest it away from destruction. It was Merton's intention to make his life a protest against everything wrong in the world: war, aggression, political tyranny, political and nationalistic propaganda and jingoism, fake political trials staged to give them the air of legitimacy, nuclear proliferation, concentration camps (no matter what euphemism they are labeled with), racial injustice, socioeconomic injustice and economic policies that only enrich the wealthy so they can lobby politicians to allow them to legally oppress people and plunder the planet.

Even in the 1960s, Merton was all too aware that many of the people who most condone the destructive actions above are people of faith, including Catholics. Merton was dismayed by our blind obedience to American nationalism that is more propaganda than history. In his "Circular Letter to Friends: "Christmas Morning—1966", Merton wrote, "we are prisoners of dead ideas and prejudices" (*The Road to Joy*). To learn more about Merton's thoughts on the Cold War, non-violence, racism, religion, and peace, it is recommended that you read *Passion for Peace,* a series of Merton's prophetic essays from the 1960s judiciously selected and arranged by his biographer, William H. Shannon.

But what could a poor monk do that would bring about "some really effective political action," as he had written to Rabbi Gendler in

A Distillation of Faith

1962? He wanted to follow Jesus's instruction to be a peacemaker, but what could he personally do to bring peace to a war-weary world? With a little help from his friends like the Berrigan Brothers, Merton formed a bold plan that might have hastened the end of the war in Vietnam. It is possible that Hanh gave Merton the names of Buddhist monasteries in South Vietnam where monks might help to smuggle him into North Vietnam on his mission of peace. A few years ago, I reached out to Hanh to ask if he had known of Merton's plans to give himself up as a peace prisoner. In his early 90s, his health was so poor that he was unable to respond. Hanh passed on January 22, 2022.

(Merton and Thich Nhat Hanh at Gethsemani, May 1966)

But regardless of who may have helped Merton to formulate his secret plan, it would not be without risks. Live or die, Merton felt it was the right course of action. In fact, he was certain of it.

Absolute Power Corrupts Absolutely

In the days before Merton embarked for Asia, he told three people that he thought he would die while on his journey. Under the shadow of the giant statue of Joseph, he told Helen Marie (Sister Mary Pius) that he thought the United States government might be responsible for his death. He specifically mentioned the C.I.A., which he feared would assassinate him to silence his public protests against the war in Vietnam. He also related his concerns to the abbot and former abbot of the monastery. Merton also hinted to others his growing concern that he was not going to return from Asia alive.

But were Merton's concerns unfounded? Would an agency of the American government assassinate an American citizen—and a renowned priest at that—while he was traveling abroad?

The answer to the question began twenty-one years earlier.

In 1947, following World War II and America's escalating tensions with Russia leading to the Cold War, Congress passed the National Security Act, establishing the Central Intelligence Agency. Secretary of State George Marshall warned President Harry Truman that the

C.I.A. would have unlimited power with virtually no governmental oversight. If he was concerned in 1947, his fears were increased a year later when Truman approved directive NSC 10/2, which authorized the newly-formed agency the powers to conduct a broad range of covert operations, all of which would be illegal violations of international laws. These covert operations would be planned and executed in such a way that the United States could deny any involvement should they be implicated, giving birth to the term "Plausible Deniability." Among the covert tasks of the agency would be assassinations, ostensibly of hostile foreign political targets with opposing ideologies, but not limited to such. This was put into practice in 1960 when, without knowledge of the President of the United States or any other elected official, the C.I.A. authorized the assassination of Fidel Castro. Recognizing that power corrupts and absolute powers corrupts absolutely, George Kennan, one of the co-sponsors of NSC 10/2 which granted the C.I.A. seemingly unbridled powers without oversight, later stated that it was the greatest mistake he ever made in his life.[3]

In 1967, four years after President John F. Kennedy's assassination (arguably by the C.I.A. using Lee Harvey Oswald as scapegoat in a plausible deniability scheme), President Johnson ordered the Inspector General's Office of the United States of America to conduct an investigation of reports that the C.I.A. had planned an assassination attempt on Cuban president, Fidel Castro in 1963, in violation of international laws. Its findings were reported in the I.G.O.'s top secret *Report on Plots to Assassinate Fidel Castro*, which described the C.I.A.'s

---

[3]From James Douglass's *JFK and the Unspeakable* (p. 33): "The CIA was now empowered to be a paramilitary organization. George Kennan, who sponsored NSC 10/2, said later in the light of history that it was "the greatest mistake I ever made." Douglass's footnote shows that he is quoting from Peter Grose, *Gentleman Spy: The Life of Allen Dulles* (New York: Houghton Mifflin, 1994, p. 293).

failed plan—code-named "Operation Mongoose"—to give Castro a diving suit lined with a poisonous fungus, and to contaminate the breathing apparatus with *Tubercle bacilli*, deadly bacteria that causes tuberculosis. If the plan had worked, Castro would have contracted tuberculosis, and he would have eventually died from it. From all outward appearances, it would have seemed that Castro died from a common disease. Assassination would not be suspected. Neither President John F. Kennedy, nor any elected member of U. S. Congress had foreknowledge of this plan, let alone sanctioned it. The C.I.A. acted on its own enterprise, with no government oversight. One can only wonder how many people have been assassinated by the C.I.A. over the years because someone inside the agency deemed some individual to be subversive, and therefore an enemy of the state. Can a person be targeted for assassination simply by getting in the way of policy? Is it possible that the C.I.A. saw Thomas Merton—a peaceful protestor whose rights were protected under the Constitution—as an enemy of the state? Did some overzealous "lone wolf" agent in the C.I.A. see Merton's Asian journey as an opportunity to get rid of a vocal dissident back home?

Dr. Marc Becker, a university professor and one of the most prominent historians to study the C.I.A., and the author of numerous books with relevant titles like *The C.I.A. in Ecuador* and *The F.B.I. in Latin America*, would disagree with my belief that the C.I.A. may have sometimes acted without directives from senior government officials. In an email he told me:

> I do not see it as rogue behavior, but as formal government policy or at least as presidential policy, because Eisenhower signed off on the 1954 coup in Guatemala, Kennedy did so for the 1961 Bay of Pigs, and probably for Operation Mongoose; President Reagan backed the contras

in their illegal war against the Sandinistas in Nicaragua, and Obama personally approved drone strikes, and given that pattern, it's fair to assume that [President] Trump approved paramilitary terrorist attacks to overthrow the constitutionally elected government in Venezuela this past summer (2020).

That's a complaint that some [people] have made: that the agency started as a place to centralize intelligence gathering but turned into a personal covert action arm of the presidency (often without congressional or broader oversight). My problem is not that the C.I.A. acts in an unrestrained, unchecked manner, but that it is an integral part of U.S. imperial policy. So, if you ask me, what you suggest is not at all out of the realm of possibility. Undoubtedly, the C.I.A. did engage in such behavior.

In his email, Dr. Becker reminded me of other occasions when the C.I.A. may have attempted to eliminate enemies of the state. He mentioned Patrice Lumumba, the hero of Congolese independence and a broader Pan-African movement toward independence, who was executed in January of 1961 in what *The Guardian* called "the most important assassination of the twentieth century." Becker related the U.S. plot to assassinate Lumumba, but acknowledged "that his domestic enemies may have got to him first."

But were foreign political figures the only assassination targets? Could a United States citizen—someone like Thomas Merton—be targeted for assassination if they got in the way of policy?

In our communication, Becker related the story of Frank Olson, an American biological warfare scientist who in November of 1953 may have been covertly dosed with LSD by his colleague, Sidney Gottlieb, who was head of the C.I.A.'s MKUltra program, a top secret research project to produce biochemical methods of mind control. A few days later, Olson "allegedly threw himself out of a closed window at the Statler Hotel" in New York City. At the request of his family, Olson's body was exhumed in 1994. An autopsy revealed that he had suffered a blow to the head *before* he had fallen from the window. To learn more about the topic, Becker recommends reading Stephen Kinzer's *Poisoner in Chief: Sidney Gottlieb and the C.I.A. Search for Mind Control.*

It has been widely speculated that the C.I.A. may have orchestrated the assassination of President John F. Kennedy in 1963 and the assassinations of Robert Kennedy and Martin Luther King, Jr., in 1968. As further evidence that the United States government may have assassinated American citizens in the 1960s, in February 2021—around the time this book was being completed—a letter was released to the public. A sort of death-bed confession by a retired Black N.Y.P.D. cop who was personally involved in Malcolm X's assassination, the letter strongly supports the notion that Malcolm X's assassination at Harlem's Audubon Ballroom on February 21, 1965 may have been a conspiracy involving the N.Y.P.D. and the F.B.I. or the C.I.A. Perceiving the outspoken Malcolm X to be a threat, the F.B.I. had been surveilling him since the 1950s. In an interview in the *New York Times* published shortly before his death, Malcolm X mentioned Patrice Lumumba, the aforementioned Congolese leader who had been the target of assassination by the C.I.A. four years earlier in 1961.

Taken altogether, is it really that difficult to believe that the C.I.A. may have assassinated Thomas Merton while he was traveling abroad in Southeast Asia during the height of the Vietnam War, and made his death look like the result of a freak accident or natural causes—as they had planned to do for Fidel Castro with Operation Mongoose in 1963?

It is no far reach of the imagination.

The year before he died, Thomas Merton urged Martin Luther King, Jr. to lend his voice to protesting the war in Vietnam, not only to advocating for civil rights. It took some convincing, but on April 4, 1967, exactly one year before his assassination, King gave a speech at Riverside Church in which he called for an end to the unjust war in Vietnam. It was reported that, should he have lived, King was going to call for the burning of draft cards in protest of the war. (In 1971, King posthumously won a Grammy Award for Best Spoken Album for his *Why I Oppose the War in Vietnam*.) That same year, King and Merton co-nominated exiled Vietnamese Buddhist monk and peace activist, Thich Nhat Hanh, for the Nobel Peace Prize for his efforts to end the war. For his own part, Merton's last book, *Faith & Violence*, published weeks before he departed for Asia in the fall of 1968, was extremely critical of the Johnson Administration's war-mongering in Southeast Asia.

Did the two popular clerics get in the way of America's war policy and what President Dwight D. Eisenhower termed the Military-Industrial Complex, a clandestine alliance between the corporations that receive almost two-thirds of America's gross national product to manufacture the machines of war, including jet fighters and helicopters, nuclear missiles, nuclear subs, and nuclear aircraft carriers?

War is good for business when your business is war.

It's important to remember that in 1964, President Lyndon Johnson told U. S. Ambassador Henry Cabot Lodge, who was Richard Nixon's vice presidential running mate against John F. Kennedy in 1960, that he didn't want to go down in history as the American president who let another Southeast Asian country fall to communism. He was worried about the domino effect of one nation falling to communism after another and what that would mean to America's influence in the region.

Did someone in the C.I.A. decide that two meddlesome preachers—one Black and one White—were not going to get in the way of all that power and money?

Or is this mere speculation?

As stated at the beginning of this chapter, before leaving for Asia, Merton hinted his concerns about the dangers of his travel to friends. Weeks before he embarked on his fateful journey, Merton said something strange to Brother David Steindl-Rast, then a 45 year old Benedictine monk, while the two were at a workshop on prayer at Our Lady of the Redwoods Abbey, a monastic community of the Trappist branch of Cistercian nuns located in Whitethorn, California, not too far from New Camaldoli Hermitage in Big Sur, where Brother David had been a monk for fourteen years. The two monks had met at other occasions, including at the Abbey of Our Lady of Gethsemani.

Born Franz Kuno Steindl-Rast in Vienna in 1926, Brother David, who is one-quarter Jewish, spent his teen years living under Nazi occupation. Although recruited into the German Army, he did not see combat. After the war, he studied art, anthropology, and psychology, earning a master's degree from the Vienna Academy of Fine Arts. In 1952, he received a Ph.D. from the University of Vienna. The next year, he moved to America, where he joined a newly-founded Catholic Benedictine community in Elmira, New York. He later served as a postdoctoral fellow at nearby Cornell University in Ithaca. In 1967, the Vatican approved Brother David's appointment to participate in a conference to promote interfaith dialogue between Christianity and Buddhism. With similar interests, Thomas Merton and Brother David met on a few occasions to talk about the topic, including at the Abbey of Gethsemani. Helen Marie (Sister Mary Pius) remembered meeting him during one of his visits. In 1968, Brother David co-founded the Center for Spiritual Studies. In 2000, he co-founded the Network for Grateful Living, for which he still serves as a senior advisor. A renowned author and lecturer, Br. David "retired" in 2018 at the age of 93 and moved to a monastery in Austria to focus on his own writing projects.

Just before the Covid-19 pandemic closed down most foreign travel, Br. David travelled to Argentina for a brief visit, but unfortunately because of travel restrictions imposed after his arrival, he was stuck for the duration of the lockdown. Always grateful, Br. David enjoyed the warm South American weather over what would have certainly been a cold winter back in Austria.

In a series of emails, Br. David told me that while he was sitting around a campfire one evening with a few other workshop participants, Tom—as Merton's friends called him—was talking about his travel plans when his voice turned grave and he asked Br. David and the others to pray for him. Merton said that what he was about to embark on was going to be very dangerous. He was worried about his safety. At the time, Brother David thought that he meant the usual dangers of foreign travel, especially to places so far away and exotic as India and Thailand. He imagined Merton meant the usual pitfalls of foreign travel: dysentery, cholera, robbery, getting lost, or losing a passport.

Brother David wondered why Merton had used such an ominous word to describe a trip he had so keenly anticipated for so long. No one there knew anything about Merton's plan to influence public sentiment against the war by surrendering himself to the North Vietnamese as a peace prisoner. Although Brother David wondered what his friend had meant at the time, he understood better months later when news of Merton's death reached America. For the last half century, Brother David wondered how it was that Thomas Merton knew that he might not return from Asia alive. After I related Merton's clandestine plan as described to me by Helen Marie Grimes, Brother David replied that it all finally made sense.

Pieces of a Puzzle

As stated at the beginning of this book I only know that the story I have told here supports the notion that Thomas Merton may have been assassinated and that he knew before he left on his Asian Journey that his travels might end with his death, one way or another. He even had an idea of who his assassin(s) might be. He said as much. From interviews and documents, we know that in the days before he left for Asia, Thomas Merton told Helen Marie (Sister Mary Pius) that he planned to sneak into North Vietnam after his conference in Bangkok ended on December 15th, and to surrender himself to the North Vietnamese as a "peace prisoner" or "hostage for peace" to help bring about an end to the unjust war that had gone on needlessly for so long, and with no end in sight, and with so many human casualties on both sides. According to the U. S. National Archives, more than 21,000 American soldiers died in Vietnam between January 1, 1969 and the end of the war. The North Vietnamese people suffered many times more deaths. If Merton had succeeded in his plan, how many of those lives might have been saved?

The question that preoccupied Merton's mind during the hot summer of 1968 was: *Wasn't the life of one poor monk worth sacrificing for the lives of tens of thousands?*

But Helen Marie wasn't the only person with whom Merton had discussed his secret plan.

During dinner at the Bristol Bar & Grill in Louisville in late January 2016, Paul Pearson reported that Jim Forest had told him that Daniel or Philip Berrigan might have first put the notion into Merton's head. As further evidence that this "hostage for peace" idea was on Merton's mind the year before he died, Michael Mott references a May 10, 1967 entry from Merton's restricted journals. Mott wrote, in his Pulitzer Prize nominated biography, *The Seven Mountains of Thomas Merton* (1983):

> "[Daniel Berrigan and Thomas Merton] talked of a number of things, including the increase of violence in the antiwar movement and also Vietnam itself. Berrigan was now anxious to make himself available as a 'hostage for peace.' Merton had had the same idea since his correspondence with [W.H.] Ferry about the Christmas truce the winter before." (p. 483)

In his "Homily at the Mass for Father M. Louis (Thomas Merton)" delivered the day after Merton died (December 11, 1968), Abbot Flavian said that Merton had a "secret prayer." He mentioned that Merton had spoken to him before he left saying that he believed he might die in Asia, and that at first the abbot thought Merton was joking but he came to understand that he was deadly serious. We know that during a private meeting sometime in March 1969, both Abbot Flavian and Abbot Fox confirmed to Sister Mary Pius and Brother Irenaeus that Thomas Merton had told them of his secret plan to surrender himself to the North Vietnamese to help bring about an end to the war. We know that in Merton's mimeographed "Farewell Letter" to friends in the fall of 1968 he stated that he did not know when he would return home to America, and he specifically mentioned that "he had no intention of going anywhere near Vietnam." We also know that Thomas Merton told Sister Mary Pius he purposefully added that false statement to the letter to throw anyone who might intercept his letter off track concerning his real purpose, particularly the F.B.I. or C.I.A.

We know we can trust Helen Marie's account of her two-year friendship with Thomas Merton. Besides the fact that she and her husband, former Br. Irenaeus, had been safeguarding Merton's possessions for half a century, there's the letter from Br. Benedict to John Howard Griffin in the fall of 1971 independently confirming the relationship and the essential facts of her story. Photographs of Br. Irenaeus and Sister Mary Pius together at Gethsemani taken by Merton himself also lend weight to Helen Marie's accounts. A handwritten note from Merton to the little nun attests to their close friendship.

There is no refuting the fact that throughout 1967 and 1968, Sister Mary Pius (Helen Marie) was exactly where she said she was and doing what she said she was doing.

We know that two men once waited along the road to his hermitage to waylay him. Merton wrote about it, and he told Brother Irenaeus and Sister Mary Pius that he thought the men looked like F.B.I. agents, "G-Men" as they used to be called. After the incident, Merton asked his brother monks to keep a lookout for strangers in their midst. Merton was convinced the government was surveilling him, most likely because of his connections to the Berrigan Brothers and others that the government considered to be subversive, like Martin Luther King, Jr, with whom Merton had planned a spiritual retreat at the Abbey of Gethsemani during the summer to discuss non-violent protest regarding Civil Rights and the war in Vietnam. But King was assassinated before the scheduled retreat. Merton and

Coretta Scott King exchanged letters of condolence. I have seen the originals. According to Helen Marie, and Paul Pearson, it was Merton who persuaded Martin Luther King, Jr. to nominate the Vietnamese monk and peace activist, Thich Nhat Hanh, for the Nobel Peace Prize in 1967, for his efforts to end the brutal war in his home country. Imagine how much that would have frustrated the Johnson Administration, especially if Hanh had received the award. In the years before his death, Merton had exchanged letters with Ethel Kennedy, Robert Kennedy's wife. Merton's final public lecture, delivered at the conference in Bangkok, included the word "Marxism" in the title, a daring move in the middle of the Cold War with all its anti-Communism sentiments. For a variety of reasons, it is likely that agents of the United States government were keeping an eye on Thomas Merton.

We know from the last book published during his life, *Faith & Violence*, that Thomas Merton was keenly aware of the life and death of Franz Jägerstätter, the Austrian peasant farmer who surrendered his life for his stance against the Nazi war machine. Merton viewed Jägerstätter as a modern day martyr, something the Catholic Church would only recognize decades later, thanks in part to Merton and his friend, Gordon Zahn. Helen Marie said Merton was talking about Jägerstätter when the photograph on the cover of this book was taken during one of their Sunday picnics after Mass. I do not think it a coincidence that *Faith & Violence*, with its poignant chapter on Jägerstätter, was published just before Merton embarked on a journey that he himself called "dangerous" and from which he told several people, including both abbots, that he might not return. To my thinking, Merton left the chapter as a breadcrumb, a compass that pointed in the direction of his motive for going to Asia in the first place. Merton was also reading the writings of Dietrich Bonhoeffer, another victim of the Nazis and a fellow clergy with profound con-

Pieces of a Puzzle

science and civil courage who once stood at a similar crossroad in his life and contemplated the only course of action.

Further, we know that during the last years of his life, Merton was keenly interested in the writings of early church figures like Origin, Tertullian, Cyprian, and especially in writers like Meister Eckhart, who insisted that followers of Jesus Christ must not kill other people and that only by *action* that saves and uplifts our fellow humanity—not simply by prayer and pious ritual—do we demonstrate our Love for God. He suggested as much in his "Farewell Letter" when he wrote about the usual protests against the war, "Will they by now have lost any usefulness?"

We know that the day before his death, Merton reported that the door to his bungalow had been unlocked when he returned and that someone had rearranged the things in his room.

We know from Fr. Matthew Fox that a former C.I.A. agent posted in Bangkok in 1968 admitted that the C.I.A. killed Merton. We know from Dr. Marc Becker—who has studied the subject for decades—that the C.I.A. did engage in such behavior in the 1960s. We also know that retired Abbot Fox (Fr. James) wrote to Merton in October while he was in India in what essentially reads as a goodbye letter, despite the fact that Merton's itinerary indicated he would be home by Christmas, as soon as the conference in Bangkok was over. Why did Abbot Fox feel the need to reconcile his 27-year relationship with Merton at that time, unless he was privy to Merton's secret plan and felt that he might never again get a chance to say what he needed to say to the man?

In another coincidence too big to ignore, in the months before he embarked on his Asian Journey, Thomas Merton finalized an agreement with Bellarmine University (then Bellarmine College) to establish the Merton Legacy Trust, naming the college as the repository of his manuscripts, letters, journals, photographs, drawings, audio-recordings, and other memorabilia *in perpetuity*. The Thomas Merton Center was established a year or two after his death. Although he had been working on the deal for years, the timing seems to support the notion that Merton was tying up loose ends before he left for Asia, in the event he did not return.

Then there's the question of why Merton asked Brother David Steindl-Rast and others sitting around a campfire at Redwoods Abbey, weeks before he left for Asia, to pray for him for fear that his trip would be "dangerous." Merton said something else during the conference at Redwoods that resonated with his conviction that love and compassion, mercy and peace require action, and that any profession of faith must be bound up with the struggle against injustice and inhumanity. He said, "Nothing that anyone says is that important." As he wrote in a journal in July 1961, Merton was sick and tired of "sincerity in righting America's wrongs that only serves to enable the individual to feel concern without doing anything." Doing something is what mattered. As John Lewis—who carried Merton's autobiography in his backpack as he crossed the Edmund Pettus Bridge—said, sometimes you need "to get into good and necessary trouble." For Merton as for Lewis, sometimes a person has to take risks to make a difference.

Taken together, the assembled evidence strongly suggests that Thomas Merton, a Catholic priest, died in that ancient and most revered of Christian traditions, as commanded by Jesus himself: to be a peacemaker (Matthew 5:9) and to lay down one's life, for friends or otherwise (John 15:13), and that he did so willingly out of love for his fellow man, for all mankind. It's too easy for us to say we'd give up our life to save others. The truth is few of us would actually do something so selfless. That's why heroes and martyrs stand out in history, because such acts of altruism are so rare. They are the best of us. They made the ultimate sacrifice, oftentimes for absolute strangers.

In his foreword, Paul Pearson rightfully mentions Merton's epiphany on that amazing afternoon in March 1958 as he stood on the corner of Fourth and Walnut in Louisville and realized that there are no strangers—that God loves every one of us equally, and that we are all shining with the Light of God (from *Conjectures of a Guilty Bystander*, 1966). He said as much in a letter to African American author and social critic, James Baldwin, shortly after his ecstatic experience: "I am therefore not completely human until I have found myself in my African and Asian and Indonesian brother because he has the part of humanity which I lack." Merton's love extended to the Vietnamese. In a poem written around the same time, Merton called Thich Nhat Hanh, the exiled Vietnamese Buddhist monk, his brother. The burning question for Merton, then, was how can we continue killing our brothers in Vietnam?

Even though Merton lived in closed cloister, largely isolated from the world, he understood that contemplatives must still be part of the world, and that faith comes only by living completely in the world, not apart from it. Merton recognized that the sufferings and problems of the world in all their variations, experiences, and perplexities are the concern of any individual who claims to be a Child of God.

By the fall of 1968, Thomas Merton realized God's all-encompassing love for every human being. His street-corner epiphany of how fully God dwells in every person was an ecstatic experience that filled him with love and changed him, the way such experiences always change the experiencer. Like few others before him, Merton came to realize that God is not a noun.

God is not a thing.

God is a verb.

God is a call to action.

Thomas Merton wanted to answer the call to action. He wanted to be a peacemaker as Jesus requires of his followers.

His decision may have cost him his life.

And yet, for various reasons such as the lingering and erroneous belief among some Catholics that Merton might have been abandoning Christianity for Buddhism, or that he was too liberal, or because he advocated for the rights of African Americans, the Catholic Church has failed to fully recognize his selfless sacrifice. It is my greatest hope that Pope Francis, who said that Merton inspired him as a young priest—and who praised him as one of the greatest Americans alongside Abraham Lincoln, Martin Luther King, Jr., and Dorothy Day—will initiate steps towards recognizing that Thomas Merton died a martyr in attempt to save tens of thousands of lives needlessly lost in an unjust war. He did so willingly and out of an abundance of love for every human being, and in fulfillment of Jesus's obligation to seek peace.

Afterword

For years after I met Helen Marie in the spring of 2015, I drove down to Lee's Summit monthly, to interview her and to take her grocery shopping or to lunch, or to fix little things around the house like a clogged sink or toilet, or to replace light bulbs that were high enough to require the use of a ladder. I always worried she wasn't eating enough. On warm days, I sometimes rode my motorcycle. It was about 400 miles round-trip. I sometimes brought friends, especially clergy who had heard about the story and wanted to meet the former nun. Sometimes we'd meet at her house. At other times, I would meet Helen Marie and her friend and neighbor, Jack, for lunch at a nearby Burger King. The get-togethers gave me a chance to further interview Helen Marie, to ask for clarification regarding things she had said or given to me, and to ask her to review and sign official documents and legal agreements related to the disposition of the Thomas Merton Collection. One of those documents was a sworn affidavit attesting to the facts as they are presented herein (the affidavit, along with photographs of the signing, is now part of the archives at the Thomas Merton Center). Jack often served as a witness when Helen Marie signed such documents.

(The author interviewing Helen Marie in July 2015 about a group photo of all the monks, including Merton and Br. Irenaeus, in the new Chapter Room at Gethsemani—taken after Fr. Flavian became the new abbot in January 1968. Photo by Amber Johnson. Used with permission)

My wife, an archaeologist, university professor, and department chair of Sociology, Anthropology, and Justice Systems at Truman State University—and the protégé and widow of the late Lewis Binford, a member of the National Academy of Science who is widely considered "the Father of Modern Archaeology"—also came along to help interview Helen Marie. During our many interviews, I video-and-audio-recorded freely and took meticulous contemporaneous notes. In January of 2016, Helen Marie even stayed with us in our home, the day before we all left together to attend the first public exhibit of artifacts from the Grimes-Smelcer Thomas Merton Collection at the Frazier Museum in Louisville.

Afterword

(The author's wife, Dr. Amber Johnson, interviewing Helen Marie in her home in July 2015)

Shortly after I first met Helen Marie, she was diagnosed with a progressive form of throat cancer. The prognosis was not good. As anticipated, the harsh chemotherapy and radiation treatments made her hair fall out (see photo at end of this book). She also lost weight and looked frail. Coinciding with her treatment was the onset of dementia. Since she was in her mid-80s, it may not have been related to the medical treatment. Either way, her mental health declined quickly and markedly. Throughout the ordeal, Helen Marie remained as joyful as ever. She often told me that she talked to her cancer, telling it that she wasn't going to let it beat her. Many times, she said, "Go away, Cancer. I don't believe in you." Often, Helen Marie told me that she was praying to Thomas Merton to be an intercessor to plead that she be cured. She ardently believed that if she recovered completely from cancer she could claim that Thomas Merton had performed a miracle, and she could ask The Vatican to initiate efforts toward beatification, a first step in the process of being declared a saint.

In fact, in less than two years, Helen Marie's doctor said her cancer was in remission. However, her dementia continued to progress. During one visit in March or April of 2018, I was pretty sure she didn't know who I was, though she was as kind and loving and cheerful as ever. Her long-term memories remained somewhat intact, though I no longer accepted what she told me on face value. For instance, a year after taking possession of the Merton Collection, I got a tattoo of Merton's laundry tag on my right leg as a remembrance of the remarkable experience. If you recall, one of the chief identifiers that proved the provenance of the artifacts was the fact that Merton's laundry tag with his number "127" was sewn onto almost every article of clothing or religious apparel in the trunks. I was wearing shorts during that hot August visit. When Helen Marie saw the tattoo, she exclaimed, "Oh, my! You have a tattoo of my old number from when I was a nun in a monastery in Brooklyn." Needless to say, her dementia was starting to cloud even her long-term memories. My own mother was suffering from the early stages of dementia around the same time. I eventually gained a great deal of insight about the inexorable destructive power of dementia and Alzheimer's—cruel diseases that take and take—thieves of memories.

In her dementia, Helen Marie became an easy target of elder fraud. Scammers preyed on her kindness and naiveté. They robbed her of her life savings. At times, her kitchen table was piled high with mail asking her for money or promising that she had won some mega-lottery, but she would have to pay the taxes in advance. She told me she didn't want the money for herself; she wanted to donate it to charities, especially to those that helped animals. She loved animals. She always had a dish of water and cat food on her front porch for any stray cats. Many a time, Helen Marie broke down in tears while confessing her shame for having been so easily duped by the scammers. She would plead with me not to tell her brother. But he already knew. He and I had spoken about it on several occasions. Precautions were being taken to protect her and her assets. For example, friends were instructed not to give Helen Marie stamps so that she would not be able to reply in letters to the scammers or to send them money.

By the fall of 2018, it was clear that Helen Marie could no longer live alone. She hadn't been feeding herself properly and regularly. She increasingly exhibited the classic signs of dementia, including delusion and paranoia. She thought neighbors were breaking into her house and taking things or hiding them from her, little things. My mother was experiencing the same kind of paranoid delusions: she frequently called or texted me complaining that people were breaking into her basement. I'd show her that all of the basement windows were fixed and could not be opened, and that the only door into the basement was made of metal and was permanently barricaded closed with a two-by-six across it, bolted into the cement walls on either side. Further, in order to reduce drafts and heat loss, the edges of the door-jam were sealed with gray duct tape, which had not been disturbed. But it was no use. No matter how many times I showed her, my mother insisted that people were breaking into the basement to get her. I recall one snowy day she called to tell me there were people outside looking in through her windows. I took her outside and showed her that there were no footprints in the snow beneath any of the windows. Despite the overwhelming evidence (or lack thereof), my mother insisted that she saw someone peering through the window. This happened several times. More than once, she asked me to get her a gun so she could shoot prowlers outside. I worried for the safety of postal workers delivering mail to her house, or anyone else strolling by. I worried for my own safety. For fear that she might have acquired a gun without my knowledge, I began to stand to the side whenever I knocked on her door or rang the doorbell.

During several visits to Helen Marie, I had brief conversations about her mental state with Jack. He was also concerned about Helen Marie's deteriorating condition. During one visit, I had called her on my cell phone just a few minutes before arriving in Lee's Summit to let her know I would be at her house soon. But when I arrived, Jack and I couldn't find her anywhere. She had wandered away. We eventually found her raking a neighbor's backyard.

Sometime around Christmas 2018, Helen Marie moved away. With help, I am told, she gained ten pounds or more in no time at all. Jack reported to me that Helen Marie thinks she's simply on vacation and will soon return home to Lee's Summit. The truth is her house has been sold, her furniture and other possessions hawked at garage sales or donated to the local Salvation Army or tossed into one of those big metal garbage dumpsters. The Grimes-Smelcer Thomas Merton Collection might have ended up in a dumpster if I hadn't come along before the cancer and dementia set in.

Jack and I continue to communicate every few months. Similarly aged to Helen Marie, Jack's health is also deteriorating.

At Helen Marie's insistence, I kept only one artifact from the two trunks—one of the three silk ties Merton had bought on the bustling streets of Bangkok in the days before he died. They had returned to the abbey with his corpse and other objects, like the white cassock and black scapular he wore during his visits with the Dalai Lama. Paul Pearson once told me that there's a photograph of Merton wearing the tie in Bangkok (Fr. Say, Merton's bungalow mate at the con-

Afterword

ference in Bangkok, may have taken the photo). I'd love to have a copy of it. Helen Marie pleaded that I should wear the tie whenever I spoke publicly about Merton. I have been faithful to her wishes. You can see me wearing it in the photographs of me, Helen Marie, Archbishop Kurtz, and Bellarmine University President, Joseph McGowan, taken at the Frazier Museum in January of 2016. I also wore it during my lecture at Truman State University. The other two silk ties went to the Thomas Merton Center at Bellarmine University.

Helen Marie was invited to attend my first public lecture about the artifacts in the trunks, which was held at Truman State University in October of 2015, but she had to cancel at the last moment because her oncologist wanted her to stay close to home in case of emergency. In lieu of her presence, Helen Marie asked me to video-record her speaking about Thomas Merton so she could thank the audience for their admiration of her dear, departed friend. Years later, she asked me to post it online so that people who read this book could view her message of love and gratitude. Click on *https://www.youtube.com/watch?v=NoWqeOfa_po* to watch the brief video.

I remember how sad I felt the morning Paul Pearson took the trunks full of Merton's possessions back to Louisville. I felt like my little role in preserving Thomas Merton's legacy had come to an end. But I was wrong. A couple years later, I made another "discovery" about Thomas Merton. Like finding the artifacts in the trunks in a garage outside Kansas City, this discovery was also purely by chance. I was researching the writings of Gwendolyn Brooks, the first African American poet to win the Pulitzer Prize for Poetry in 1950. My longtime co-editor at *Rosebud* magazine, Rod Clark, had been a student of hers at the University of Wisconsin-Madison in the 1970s, and we published a poem of hers after her death in 2000.

In my research, I stumbled upon a curious letter from Columbia University's Pulitzer Prize Advisory Committee. The letter indicated the committee's choice of Ms. Brooks to receive the prestigious award, but it also included their rationale. More interestingly to me, the letter listed the names of seven other poetry books the committee had considered for the prize. At the bottom of the short list was *The Tears of the Blind Lions* by Thomas Merton (New Directions, 1948). It turns out, I have learned, that Thomas Merton never knew that one of his poetry books had been a contender for the Pulitzer Prize. In fact, not even his publisher knew. Half a century after his death, no scholar of Merton's life and works had ever heard about it until Paul Pearson and I published our co-written article, "Thomas Merton and the Curious Case of the 1950 Pulitzer Prize" in *Bellarmine*, the official magazine of Bellarmine University where the Thomas Merton Center is housed.

An unforeseen event impacted the history of this story. In early 2020, a novel coronavirus called Covid-19 became a global pandemic. It reached America's shores in March. By Thanksgiving, as many as 200,000 new cases were reported every single day. By Christmas, the United States had over ten million confirmed cases of infection, the most of any country in the world, and by the time I finished the rough draft of this book in March 2021—the one year "anniversary" of the pandemic—the death toll was 550,000—more than the loss of all American soldiers in WWII and Vietnam combined. By the summer of 2021, more transmissible and more deadly mutations of the virus were beginning to appear around the world. By the late fall of 2021, over 800,000 Americans had perished from Covid-19, mostly because of the polarizing anti-vax political climate. At the current rate, the number of American deaths will surely surpass a million by the time this book comes out. Inexcusably, more Americans died from Covid-19 than from the 1918 Spanish Flu which happened during a time when medicine and science could not manufacture a highly effective and safe vaccine as we have nowadays. The elderly like Helen Marie, now 90 years old, were especially vulnerable. But the virus took the lives of younger folks as well, folks my age, young adults, and even children. The virus didn't care about your faith or politics. It didn't care if you were rich or poor (though the rich can afford better healthcare and to work remotely, thereby practicing social distancing). It didn't care if you believed in it or not. It infected and killed indiscriminately.

Increasingly, it crossed my mind that I could die from the virus. I had nightmares worrying about it. I didn't want to leave my wife without a husband and my daughters without a father. But it also worried me that, should I die, Helen Marie's secret—the one she had safeguarded for half a century and had entrusted to me—might never be told. Although I had shared portions of the manuscript with a few people, I had not disclosed Helen Marie's secret to anyone. I kept a lot of information close to the vest. I once asked Helen Marie why she had never told her story about Merton's peace-maker plan to some friend who might have written it down. She replied that until I came along, she never knew anyone with the interest and the ability to write and publish her story, and so she held it inside, hoping and praying. Over and over, she expressed her belief that Thomas Merton had sent me in answer to her prayers. The realization that Helen Marie's account could be lost forever if I died spurred me to finish a draft of this book, which my wife or someone like Paul Pearson could edit and publish posthumously on my behalf. To be honest, sometimes I think Helen Marie's story would have been better served if she had told it to Paul instead of to me.

Sadly, Helen Marie passed away in her sleep in mid-January, 2022.

Looking back now, I am grateful for that morning in the spring of 2015, when I was sitting at that cafeteria booth working on a different book with one of Thomas Merton's books laying face-up on the table for passersby to see—for that moment propelled me on this amazing journey. They say timing is everything. If I had met Helen Marie even a couple years later, those trunks full of Merton's possessions might have ended up in the landfill and her amazing story might have been lost forever. From my experience, I have come to admire Merton even more. Helen Marie frequently said she believed Merton had sent me to her doorstep in answer to her prayers. I don't know if that's true, but if it is, her old friend and mentor must have known it was the right time.

If I learned anything else from my remarkable journey, it is that in light of current events—specifically yet another unjust war with untold human suffering—Thomas Merton's protests against war, nuclear proliferation, racism, and social injustice in the 1960s are as relevant today as they were back then. The world needs more people like Thomas Merton who are willing to take risks to put their love into action.

Help Spread the Word

If this book affected you or deepened your faith, please help spread the word. This story about peace and compassion and selflessness deserves to be shared. Give it as a gift to friends and relatives, young and old alike. Buy a copy for your local library. Write a book review for your local newspaper or church newspaper or newsletter, radio station, or favorite magazine. Write a review on amazon.com or goodreads.com or elsewhere. Talk about it on Facebook. Tweet about it. Post a YouTube video or blog about it. Send an Instagram of the book cover. Ask your local librarian to recommend it. Ask your local bookseller to stock it. Discuss it in book clubs and Bible study groups. Encourage its translation into other languages. The success of a book depends on readers like you who recommend it to their friends and others.

Invite the Author to Speak

The author appreciates the opportunity to travel and to speak about Thomas Merton and especially about his amazing and unlikely spiritual journey as it related to the discovery and disposition of the Grimes-Smelcer Thomas Merton Collection. Dr. Smelcer has created an informative public lecture filled with photographs and related documents. Besides, it would give him a chance to wear Thomas Merton's old silk tie, the one he bought in Bangkok in the days before he died. To inquire about the opportunity or contact the author, go to *www.johnsmelcer.com* and click on "contact."

Works Cited

A Hand of Peace: Pope Pius XII and the Holocaust [film]. Written and directed by David Naglieri. Salt and Light Television Production, 2008, in association with Ignatius Press, 2009.

A Hidden Life. [DVD] Written and directed by Terence Malick. Twentieth Century Fox Home Entertainment, 2020. (This is for the DVD, I think the film was released in 2019.)

Becker, Marc. Personal Communications. November 26, 2020.

Benedict, Brother. Personal Letter to John Howard Griffin. August 20, 1971.

Bonhoeffer, Dietrich. *Letters & Papers from Prison.* New York: Simon & Schuster, 1997.

Burns, Fr. M. Flavian (Abbot). "Homily at the Mass for Father M. Louis (Thomas Merton)." Abbey of Gethsemani. December 11, 1968. Online at *http://merton.org/50th/Burns-Homily-12-11-68.pdf*

Douglass, James. *JFK and the Unspeakable.* New York: Scribner's, 2008.

———. Personal Communications, April-May 2018.

Einstein, Albert. *The World as I See It*. Secaucus: Citadel Press, 1979.

Fox, Matthew. *A Way to God: Thomas Merton's Creation Spirituality Journey*. Navato: New World Library, 2016.

——. Personal Communications, April 2018 - March 2021.

Franz Jägerstätter: A Man of Conscience [film]. Directed by Jason Schmidt and Ron Schmidt. Hope Media Productions, 2009.

Griffin, John Howard, *Follow the Ecstasy: Thomas Merton, The Hermitage Years, 1965-1968*. Fort Worth: JHG Editions/Latitudes Press, 1983.

——. *Black Like Me*. New York: Houghton Mifflin, 1961.

King, Martin Luther, Jr. *Why We Can't Wait*. New York: Harper & Row, 1964.

Kinzer, Stephen. *Poisoner-in-Chief: Sidney Gottlieb and the C.I.A. Search for Mind Control*. New York: Henry Holt, 2019.

McCullough, David. *The Johnstown Flood*. New York: Simon & Schuster, 1968.

Merton: A Film Biography [VHS video]. New York: First Run Features/NOS Television Holland, 1984.

Merton, Thomas. *The Asian Journal of Thomas Merton*. New York: New Directions, 1973.

——. *Conjectures of a Guilty Bystander*. Garden City: Double Day, 1966.

——. *Faith & Violence*. Notre Dame University Press, 1968.

——. "Farewell Letter." Mimeograph copy. Fall 1968.

———. *Gethsemani: A Life of Praise*. Abbey of Gethsemani Press, 1966.

———. *The Literary Essays of Thomas Merton* edited by Patrick Hart. New York: New Directions, 1985.

———. "Thomas Merton's Notes on Dietrich Bonhoeffer," Bellarmine University Archives.

———. *Raids on the Unspeakable*. New York: New Directions, 1966.

———. *Seeds of Destruction*. New York: Farrar, Straus & Giroux, 1964.

———. *Tears of the Blind Lions*. New York: New Directions, 1948.

———. *The Seven Storey Mountain*. Farrar, Straus & Giroux, 1948.

———. *The Wisdom of the Desert*. Abbey of Gethsemani, 1960.

Mott, Michael. *The Seven Mountains of Thomas Merton*. Mariner Books, 1983.

Pagels, Elaine. *The Gnostic Gospels*. New York: Random House, 1989.

Pearson, Paul. Personal Communications, May 2015 – March 2021.

Shannon, William (ed.). *Passion for Peace*. Crossroads/University of Michigan, 1995.

———. *Thomas Merton, Witness to Freedom: Letters in Times of Crisis*. New York: Harcourt Brace, 1994.

Smelcer, John. "Finding Thomas Merton" in *Tikkun*, Vol. 32, Number 3, 2017.

———. "Thomas Merton: Kentucky's Uncommon Son" in *Kentucky Monthly*, May 2016.

———. NPR Interview on Discovery of Thomas Merton Artifacts, October 6, 2015. Available online at *https://www.kbia.org/news/-2015-10-05/thomas-mertons-personal-belongings-resurface-in-missouri-nearly-fifty-years-after-his-death*

———. *The Raven and the Totem: Alaska Native Myths and Legends*. Anchorage: Salmon Run Press, 1991; Kirksville: Naciketas Press, 2015.

———. *Trickster: Myths from the Ahtna Athabaskan Indians of Alaska*. Kirksville: Naciketas Press, 2016.

———. *In the Shadows of Mountains*. Glennallen: Ahtna Heritage Foundation, 1997.

———. *The Gospel of Simon*. Fredonia: Leapfrog Press, 2016.

———. *The Field* (Das Feld). Unpublished manuscript.

Smelcer, John and Paul Pearson. "Thomas Merton and the Curious Case of the 1950 Pulitzer Prize" in *Bellarmine*, Fall 2019.

Steindl-Rast, David. Personal Communications, April 2019 – December 2020.

Tracy, James. "Thomas Merton: Enemy of the Warfare State" (video). Available online at *https://heresycentral.is/jamestracy/thomas-merton-enemy-of-the-warfare-state/*

Turley, Hugh and David Martin. *The Martyrdom of Thomas Merton*. Hyattsville: McCabe Publishing, 2018.

———. "Why Catholics Haven't Heard of Thomas Merton's Elimination." *Island Catholic News*, June 14, 2019. Available online at *https://islandcatholicnews.ca/newsstory/why-catholics-havent-heard-thomas-mertons-elimination/*

U. S. National Archives, database on mortalities during Vietnam War. (Accessed February 2021)

Zahn, Gordon. *In Solitary Witness: The Life and Death of Franz Jägerstätter.* New York: Henry Holt, 1964.

About the Authors

John Smelcer, Ph.D. is the award-winning author of more than sixty books, including *The Gospel of Simon*, his poignant and daring retelling of Jesus's crucifixion as told by Simon of Cyrene, and *A New Day*, his pocketbook of meditations to inspire compassion, love, mercy, contemplation, wellbeing, social justice, and the spiritual life. His poems, stories, articles, essays, and interviews appear in hundreds of magazines worldwide. For a quarter century, John was poetry editor at *Rosebud* magazine. Nowadays, he serves as Senior Editor Emeritus. He studied literature at Cambridge and Oxford and world religions at Harvard. He is the inaugural writer-in-residence and blogger at the Charter for Compassion, established by Karen Armstrong (*A History of God*), where he teaches a popular global online course called "Poetry for Inspiration and Well-Being." He is a frequent contributor to *Tikkun*, the acclaimed Jewish magazine of interfaith discourse, peace, social justice, and environmentalism. To learn more or to contact the author click on *www.johnsmelcer.com*. (Photograph of the author and Helen Marie Grimes, c. 2016. Photo by Amber Johnson. Used with permission.)

For over twenty years, Paul M. Pearson, Ph.D. has been director of the Thomas Merton Center at Bellarmine University in Louisville, Kentucky, and chief of research for the Merton Legacy Trust. He is resident secretary of the International Thomas Merton Society and served as president for the tenth administration. He previously edited *Seeking Paradise: Merton and the Shakers* (Orbis, 2003), *A Meeting of Angels: The Correspondence of Thomas Merton* with Edward Deming and Faith Andrews (Broadstone, 2008), *Thomas Merton on Christian Contemplation* (New Directions, 2012), and *Beholding Paradise: The Photography of Thomas Merton* (Paulist Press, 2020). (Photograph of Paul Pearson by James X. Robinson. Used with permission.)

www.ingramcontent.com/pod-product-compliance
Lightning Source LLC
Chambersburg PA
CBHW022007120526
44592CB00034B/504